∞

Young and Catholic

Tim Drake

Young and Catholic

The Face of Tomorrow's Church

SOPHIA INSTITUTE PRESS®
Manchester, New Hampshire

Portions of this book appeared previously in articles in the *National Catholic Register* and are used here with the permission of the *National Catholic Register*.

Sophia Institute Press®
Box 5284, Manchester, NH 03108
1-800-888-9344
www.sophiainstitute.com

Library of Congress Cataloging-in-Publication Data

Drake, Tim, 1967-
    Young and Catholic : the face of tomorrow's church / Tim Drake.
        p. cm.
    Includes bibliographical references.
    ISBN 1-928832-93-8 (pbk. : alk. paper)
    1. Church work with youth — Catholic Church. 2. Catholic
youth — Religious life. 3. Church work with young adults. 4. Catholic
Church — History — 21st century. I. Title.
BX2347.8.Y7D72 2004
282'.73'0835 — dc22   2004017971

04 05 06 07 08 09 10 9 8 7 6 5 4 3 2 1

In memory of
Baby Gabriel Drake —
forever young

Contents

∞

Acknowledgments

First and foremost I want to thank my wife, Mary, for her many sacrifices during the year and a half it took me to write this book. Her vocation as a wife, mother, and teacher makes my vocation as a writer possible. I am grateful for her support and her keen editorial eye.

Second, I am indebted to the patience and the professional editorial skills of the staff at Sophia Institute Press. I thank them for bringing the idea for this book to me.

Finally, I am grateful to all those who were willing to be interviewed. This book would not exist without you. I am also thankful for all those who helped out at various stages and in various ways (prayer, editorial direction, and friendship) and assisted in bringing it to fruition, especially Jeff Korman.

∞

Introduction

A Reason for Hope

"I am more than hopeful. Et portae inferi non praevalebunt adversus eam. *The gates of hell are not going to close us down one bit."*

Adam Austin, 30, investment banking
analyst, Charlotte, North Carolina

∞

It's a typical Wednesday morning. Our five young children rise and, with considerable parental assistance, get dressed for the day. We drive the short distance to attend daily Mass together at our local parish. It's something we've tried to do for the past few years.

This particular morning is like all the rest. Our family of seven makes up one-fifth of the congregation. We're also the only people in the church who are younger than forty.

Every day it's the same story, and it's played out no matter which of the four local parishes we attend for morning Mass.

I ask myself, "Where are the young people?" and I wonder if the older generation gathered in the pews around me ever ask themselves the same question.

Ever since my conversion nine years ago, I've noticed this phenomenon, which I call "the graying of the pews." Sadly, it can be observed even on Sundays. There just don't seem to be many young people going to Mass.

Where can they be? It's discouraging. Is this what the future holds? Are the critical pundits right? Is the Church aging and dying in America?

In my years as a Catholic journalist I have learned that there's far more to the Church than meets the eye. Looking beyond the empty or graying pews in a given parish or city, I have discovered a ground-swell of renewal — particularly among the young — marked by zeal for Christ and fidelity to the Church and its teachings. Some parishes and even whole dioceses have already been transformed and are teeming with enthusiastic young adults, teens, and their families. Others show unmistakable signs of the dawn of being on the verge of their own transformation.

I've spoken to many youth in my own parish. I've reported on youth and young adults in the pages of the periodicals for which I write, and I've joined them when they gather to proclaim their love for Christ and his Church, particularly at World Youth Day. In preparation for writing this book, I spoke to more than three hundred young people from across the United States and elsewhere.

I've found that there are, indeed, many reasons for hope.

Teens gather by the hundreds to attend special youth Masses in parishes around the country, often on Saturday or Sunday evenings. They gather for special youth Masses in St. Paul, Minnesota, and in Phoenix, Arizona. Young adults get together to discuss theology on a Saturday night in Newark, Ohio, and to study the Holy Father's encyclicals in New York, Minneapolis, and Kansas City. Young Catholic leaders gather annually in Chicago and in Canada to network and collaborate with one another. They gather by the millions at World Youth Day, and they're active in changing international policy at the United Nations.

They are converting to the Faith in large numbers on both secular and Catholic college campuses in California, Texas, and Illinois. They are swelling the ranks of religious orders in Tennessee, Ohio, Michigan, and New York — to such an extent that some orders don't have space for all the new members. They are being ordained priests in dioceses such as Denver, Baltimore, and Lincoln.

Reasons for hope. Hope for the future of the Church.

These young Catholics desperately need our encouragement and inspiration. Facing an increasingly hostile, secularized culture, they need to know that they're not alone. The examples of others can serve to continue the New Evangelization that Pope John Paul II has promised the Church. The New Springtime has already begun. Its blossoming can be seen in the stories told in this book.

Who are these young people? What is it that draws them and motivates them to live out their Catholic Faith? What makes them different from their peers?

In this book I want to introduce you to today's young Catholics. Between the ages of sixteen and thirty-nine, they are as diverse and varied as the Church herself. Through their stories, you will come to meet them, know them, and understand what makes them tick. They are the future of the Church. These are their stories.

Speaking to the youth of Madrid in May 2003, Pope John Paul II said, "You are the hope of the Church, no less than of society. . . . I continue to believe in young people, in you."[1]

Like the Holy Father, we can rest assured. The Church of the future is in good hands.

Tim Drake
St. Cloud, Minnesota
May 1, 2004
Feast of St. Joseph the Worker

[1] Pope John Paul II, "Pope's Words to Youth in Madrid," Vatican Information Service, May 5, 2003.

∞

Young and Catholic

∞

Signs of Contradiction

Generations X and Y

"I love the awe I experience each time I receive the Holy Eucharist."

David McDonough, 27,
bartender, Chicago, Illinois

The difference could not have been starker.

It was ten p.m. on a Thursday night. Approximately seventy attendees of the 2003 Catholic Press Association conference, the overwhelming majority of them above the age of forty, were crowded into an oversize Atlanta Hilton hotel room that was still two sizes too small. Billed as the hospitality room, the gathering there was loud and raucous. Wine, beer, and mixed drinks flowed freely, as did conversation — reminiscent of a bad frat-house party populated primarily by the old guard.

Twenty-four floors below, two older attendees along with seven under the age of forty, gathered in silence. The silence, like the noise so many floors above, was deafening, as all sat or kneeled in prayer before Jesus Christ, exposed in the Blessed Sacrament during eucharistic adoration.

The comparison is drawn not to suggest that the older generation likes to drink and party and the younger group does not; in fact, the younger crowd had been partying just three hours earlier at Atlanta's Max Lager restaurant. Nor is the comparison drawn to suggest that one generation is more pious than the other.

What the story highlights is how faithful young Catholics, in many ways, are a sign of contradiction.

Foremost, the young are a sign of contradiction simply by virtue of their existence. Today's youth and young adults came of age during a time when at least one-third of their generation has been killed in the womb through legalized abortion. They stand as a testament of those deemed "worthy to live." They recognize that some of their potential friends, fellow students, coworkers and co-worshipers, and brothers and sisters were not given the opportunity they have been given.

They are signs of contradiction in other ways as well.

Unlike the previous generation, the majority of those born between 1965 and 1983 (the "Baby Busters") have known no pope other than John Paul II. They have grown up with him. Many have come to know him first through his media appearances, as well as his many travels — particularly his pilgrimages devoted to the world's youth. They are initially attracted by his witness and his charisma, and often later come to discover his writings and learn of his theology.

Young Catholics are also a sign of contradiction in the very practice of their Faith — a Faith that is often challenged daily by their peers, their teachers, the secular media, and sometimes by their own family. Whereas the previous generation came of age in a time when everyone they knew was Catholic, most attended Catholic schools, and the majority married fellow Catholics, the younger generation does not benefit from such familiarity.

Mark Huegerich, thirty-six, a television commercial producer in Des Moines, Iowa, expresses this well.

"During my twelve years of Catholic school, I recall meeting about eight people who were not Catholic," he says. "Then I went to college, got a charismatic Pentecostal roommate, and almost no one was Catholic."

In a largely secularized culture, those with an active worship or devotional life stand apart. While the previous generation may have abandoned many of the devotional practices once popular prior to the Second Vatican Council, the younger generation has rediscovered such practices as eucharistic adoration, Marian devotions, the Rosary, and the Liturgy of the Hours. They seek a deeper, more meaningful faith — a faith that is lived out not just on Sunday, but in their daily relationships and lives. Studies and polls have suggested that the younger generation possesses a weaker and more tentative affiliation with the institutional Church. They claim that significant numbers of young-adult Catholics no longer see the Church as unique or essential, the Pope as necessary, the Church's structures as important, or Tradition as a source of objective truth.[2]

Despite strong anecdotal evidence that the younger generation is trending increasingly orthodox and traditional in its practice of Christianity, major media outlets would rather report the story that youth and young adults are alienated and disengaged from the religion of their parents and grandparents. It makes for more interesting copy to report that youth are rebelling against the Church rather than embracing it.

Yet, the story behind the headlines is that large numbers of youth and young adults are embracing the Church.

According to the Barna Research Group, Ltd., eighty-six percent of teenagers claim that they're Christian. Twenty-two percent describe themselves as Catholic. Both Gallup and Barna Research have found that nearly sixty percent of teens in the United States attend a religious service weekly. Barna found that more than seven out of ten teenagers take part in some church-related effort in a typical week — whether a youth-group meeting,

---

[2] Dean Hoge, et al., *Young Adult Catholics: Religion in the Culture of Choice* (Notre Dame: University of Notre Dame Press, 2001), 219-221.

Bible-study class, or Sunday school class — a number that far exceeds the participation level among adults.[3]

For college student Sarah Bollinger, that involvement outside of Sunday services meant reaching beyond the borders of her Buford, Georgia, parish.

∞

Her Bake Sale Helped a Nation

Since 1971, Nicaragua has been devastated by civil war and natural disasters. Hurricane Mitch triggered a mudslide on the Casitas volcano in 1998, resulting in the death of more than three thousand people. Thousands of children were left abandoned. In the fall of 1997, then-high school freshman Sarah Bollinger and her youth group at Prince of Peace Catholic Church in Buford, Georgia, decided to try to help.

"We had done community service with handicapped adults and in the downtown soup kitchen," says Sarah, "but we wanted to form a bond and find something we could continue."

Through Food for the Poor, one of the youth leaders, John Bland, was connected with Fr. Marco Dessy, an Italian missionary who had worked in the town of Chinandega, Nicaragua, for thirty years.

Bland traveled to Nicaragua to explore the possibilities. He returned home with video footage to show the youth group.

"John told us that we could just be pen pals, or if we wanted, we could help raise money to build a cafeteria for the schoolchildren. They were eating outdoors near a garbage dump," explains Sarah.

"I don't remember many of the images from the video," she admits, "but that night I knew. I saw myself down there."

---

[3] George Barna, *Third Millennium Teens* (Ventura, California: Barna Research Group, Ltd., 2000).

The following summer, Fr. Dessy brought a Nicaraguan boys' choir to Prince of Peace as a fund-raiser. Moved by the choir and Fr. Dessy's appeal, Bollinger and her best friend, Jessica Kiefer, set to work.

"After Mass I asked Fr. Jimmy Adams if we could have a bake sale," recalls Sarah. "Jessica and I made a roster of sixty young people and called each of them to ask them to bring baked goods. We raised about $800."

After the bake sale, the teens organized other fund-raisers. They sold Advent wreaths, made posters and set out collection cans, and held a "buy an angel to save an angel" fund-raiser.

By April 1999, the group had raised enough money not only to build the cafeteria, but also to send nineteen teens and an equal number of adults to Chinandega for their first mission trip.

While there, Bollinger played with children, distributed food to rural areas, and helped build homes. At the inauguration of the cafeteria, Bollinger became godmother to a young Nicaraguan boy named Christian Alberto.

On the trip home, the youth leaders spoke of transforming their work into a nonprofit organization. It was then that Amigos for Christ was born. Sarah's inspiration led to the group's founding.

"She started it," says John Bland, director of Amigos for Christ. "She opened doors for hundreds of other teenagers to utilize their talents for the poor."

Amigos for Christ has expanded to New Orleans, Louisiana, and Mobile, Alabama, and has sent more than $13 million in aid to Chinandega. They have drilled twenty-five wells, completed building a surgical hospital, and are in the process of completing 170 homes.

"Words cannot describe the difference that we have made there," says Sarah.

Young and Catholic

Amigos for Christ assists the poor in Nicaragua.

The work has become her life. She has made nine mission trips to the country. In 2000 she received the Maryknoll Youth World Mission Award for her work.

Now in college, Bollinger is uncertain as to what degree she will pursue, but she is certain that she wants to do something that can aid both the United States and Nicaragua.

"I will continue to work in Nicaragua until there is no longer a need," she adds.

∞

More Evidence

Other studies have reinforced Barna's findings. In contrast to the widely held view that the young find church boring or irrelevant, a 2003 study by the London-based Christian Research group revealed that two-thirds of youth ages ten to fourteen enjoy attending church. The study also found that ninety-one percent of those who have stopped going to church continue to attend other church-based youth activities.[4]

According to a 1997 Gallup poll, nearly eighty percent of teenagers age thirteen to seventeen considered religion a significant influence on their life. A 2000 Gallup poll found that sixty-five percent of the nation's youth are "very" or "somewhat" confident that they will be more religious than their parents.

---

[4] Peter Brierley, *Reaching and Keeping Tweenagers* (London: Christian Research, 2003).

Contrary to what is commonly believed, the vast majority of older U.S. adolescents express a positive regard for organized religion. In 2004 the National Study of Youth and Religion (NSYR), in one of the most comprehensive studies of twelfth-grade students ever conducted, discovered that about two-thirds did not appear to be alienated from or hostile toward organized religion. The study found that two-thirds of them closely agree with the religious ideas of their parents. Three-fourths believe that churches and religious organizations are doing a good or fair job for the country, and seven in ten would like to see religion exert the same, more, or much more influence in society.[5]

Other NSYR reports indicate that the most important factor in the strength of a young person's religious faith is the religious practices of his parents. That's certainly true in the case of high school senior Tom Wills.

∞

Bringing Christ to the Poor

While seventeen-year-old Tom Wills' friends were hanging out at the mall and playing video games, Wills participated in a Youth for the Third Millennium Mega-Mission to help those less fortunate near Mexico City.

The senior from Burke, Virginia, admits that the mission was primarily his mother's idea, but he felt called to make the commitment during Holy Week 2003. His mother, Susan Wills, serves as assistant director for program development in the Secretariat for Pro-Life Activities with the U.S. Conference of Catholic Bishops.

---

[5] Christian Smith, et al., *Are American Youth Alienated from Organized Religion?* (Chapel Hill: National Study of Youth and Religion, 2004).

Young and Catholic

"I wanted to sacrifice something during Lent bigger than candy and video games," says Wills.

Wills didn't know what to expect, but the Friday before Palm Sunday he traveled to a tiny village in the mountains of the Puebla District of Mexico City known as Reyes Hogpan. There he joined nine high school students from a Catholic high school in Mexico City for a weeklong mission.

The team played basketball with the other boys in the village and got to know them. A weightlifter, swimmer, and football player, Wills admits that basketball was a stretch.

"It's not my best game," says Wills, "but at six-foot-one they thought I was huge just because I could block shots and dunk."

The game helped to break the ice.

"As they got to know us, they started coming to our talks," says Wills.

The team delivered presentations on topics such as the Rosary, dating and chastity, respect for life, and marriage. They taught the younger children how to pray the Rosary, and walking in pairs they visited nearly every family in the area, some as far away as an hour or two from the village.

In exchange, the families provided tortillas, beans, and coffee. Wills describes the families as the most generous people he has ever known.

"Every family was so hospitable — so glad to share what little they had," he says. "It was very moving. The people in Reyes Hogpan had hardly any possessions, and yet they were personally happier than almost everyone I know in the States."

Once the village priest, Don Antonio, asked Wills to bring the Eucharist to an old woman who lived far from the village.

"She had been bedridden for six years and was close to dying," explains Wills. "To carry Jesus all that way and see how grateful she was to receive him made me realize more deeply what an incredible gift the Eucharist is." It's a gift that Wills admitted he has sometimes taken for granted.

Wills explains that the mission was easily one of his most difficult undertakings, but also one of the most rewarding experiences he has ever had.

"I grew much closer to God and the Church and am much more appreciative of my blessings," Wills concludes.

He looks forward to future missions and has also talked his younger brother into attending.

∽

Across Ethnic Lines

This youthful attraction to the Faith is one that also appears to cross ethnic lines. Young American Latinos appear to be returning to the religion of their ancestors, attending church in greater numbers than the previous generation.[6] Thirty percent of American Catholics are Latinos, and within the next two decades Latino Catholics will constitute a majority of U.S. Catholics.[7]

Former youth minister Carlos Briceño, thirty-nine, has worked with Hispanic youth in both New York and at St. Jerome's Catholic Church in Largo, Florida. He says that there is a definite fervor among Hispanic Catholics.

"They go to Church every Sunday and they make the Sign of the Cross every time they pass a church," says Briceño.

Still, he worries about the impact of popular culture.

---

[6] Uwe Siemon-Netto, "Analysis: Young Latinos? Strong Believers," United Press International, June 26, 2003.

[7] Timothy Matovina, "Hispanic Catholics: 'El futuro' is here," Commonweal, September 14, 2001.

"I was influenced by television, but I was more influenced by my parents," he explains. "A lot of teens today aren't being influenced by their parents. They are influenced by television reality programs, movies, the Internet, and music. A lot of it is poisonous."

While there are many forces working against them, Briceño believes that light can penetrate the darkness. He gave the example of a retreat that his parish gave for the youth.

"It was entirely funded by donations from the parishioners," he says. "They donated food and money, and parishioners prayed for the teens around the clock." Fifteen teenagers attended the retreat. "Many of the kids were transformed," adds Briceño. "I've seen a lot of grace in my job."

The NSYR study also discovered that black youth are even less likely to be alienated from organized religion than white youth. Black twelfth-graders were significantly more likely than their white classmates to agree with their parents about religious beliefs, to desire more social influence for churches, and to give money or expect to give money to churches — a finding that the authors found in agreement with findings by other studies as well.[8]

African-American high school junior Tiffany Pullis of St. Cloud, Minnesota offers an example.

∞

Giving Up Her Summer Vacation

During the summer of 2003, Pullis gave up her summer vacation to organize her parish's first-ever Vacation Bible School. While many of the area's ten Catholic churches had held Vacation Bible School programs over the years, one of her community's largest

___

[8] Smith, et al., *Are American Youth Alienated from Organized Religion?*

churches, the Church of St. Anthony, had never held one. Pullis, along with fellow junior Mary Jansen — both of whom attended World Youth Day 2002 in Toronto — felt inspired to change that. "A friend from a nearby church told us about the Vacation Bible School program that they did every year," explains Pullis. "We decided that we wanted to do something, so during the summer of 2002 we attended their program to get ideas."

"A Vacation Bible School seemed like an awesome way to be with kids and bring others closer to God," says Jansen.

With planning beginning in earnest in April 2003, the teenagers spent nearly every day after school planning the activities and purchasing materials. They also recruited nearly twenty other teens to serve as leaders. In the end, thirty-two children attended the ocean-theme program.

"I have a strong faith," says Pullis, "but when I saw the children and how unafraid they were to say that they loved Jesus, I realized that their faith was even stronger. They helped teach me that we don't have to be silent about our love of God."

As a result of their work, both teens received the Girls Scouts' highest award, the Gold Award.

During the summer of 2003, Mary Jansen (right) and her friend Tiffany Pullis, then high school juniors, organized the first Vacation Bible School at St. Anthony Parish, in St. Cloud, Minnesota.

Young and Catholic

∞

Generations X and Y

Youth and young adults represent a considerable portion of today's Church and the leadership of tomorrow's Church. With a total U.S. Catholic population of 66.4 million, the Catholic cohort between the ages of eighteen and forty make up approximately one-third of the total at roughly 22 million.

Colleen Carroll, in her book *The New Faithful*, explains that although not everyone in the age group born between 1965 and 1983 is religiously oriented, those who are tend to be more traditional in their beliefs and morality — sharing a rich devotional life, a deep affection for Pope John Paul II, and a tendency to hold traditional stances on doctrinal and moral issues.

Carroll points out, for example, that among Catholic priests, the youngest are as traditional as the oldest. Growing numbers of married couples in this age group tend to reject artificial contraception, and increasing numbers of young singles are embracing premarital chastity.

Papal biographer George Weigel notes, "Young men and women, formed in the image of John Paul II and joyfully living the Catholic sexual ethic, are filling graduate departments of theology and philosophy at Catholic universities."[9]

Rather than rejecting authority, these young adults seek authoritative guidelines and meaningful commitments. Across the spectrum, Catholic youths are manifesting dynamic orthodoxy, a personal relationship with Christ, and a deep love for the Church and the Holy Father.

---

[9] George Weigel, *The Courage to Be Catholic: Crisis, Reform, and the Future of the Church* (New York: Basic Books, 2002), 223.

Indeed, even those who have offered evidence for the younger generation's alienation from the Faith have admitted as such. In the study *Young Adult Catholics: Religion in the Culture of Choice*, the authors note:

> Most young adults like being Catholic and cannot imagine themselves being anything other than Catholic. The overwhelming majority see the sacraments . . . as essential to the Catholic Faith. Most consider themselves spiritual, pray regularly, and support the Church's social mission. . . . They see Catholicism as the oldest and most central expression of Christianity. . . . Many young adult Catholics also take pride in the global dimensions of Catholicism and in the media visibility of a pope whose personal integrity and firmness on moral and ethical questions are admired and respected. . . .[10]

The American bishops recognize this fact as well. In 1996 the U.S. Conference of Catholic Bishops' Secretariat for Family, Laity, Women, and Youth released a pastoral plan directed specifically at young Catholics. Titled *Sons and Daughters of the Light: A Pastoral Plan for Ministry with Young Adults*, the document recognizes the tremendous gift that the young bring to Church life and the spiritual hunger of young adults, and sets forth specific goals for spiritual formation and direction, religious education, and vocation discernment for young people.[11]

The past decade has witnessed a marked increase in parish efforts to reach youth. This is evidenced through the increasing

---

[10] Dean Hoge, et al., *Young Adult Catholics*, 218.

[11] National Conference of Catholic Bishops/U.S. Catholic Conference of Bishops, *Sons and Daughters of the Light: A Pastoral Plan for Ministry with Young Adults* (Washington, D.C.: United States Catholic Conference, 1996).

number of youth ministry programs found in local parishes, as well as by the rise of several national Catholic youth ministry programs. Not only is the Church attempting to connect with the young, but the youth appear to be responding.

Contrary to popularly held public opinion, Catholic young adults do care about their religion. They demonstrate a deep passion and enthusiasm for the Faith not often seen in the previous generation. By embracing the Church, they are expressing their desire for a religion that is lived out and has the power to transform. For many teens, Sundays are not enough.

∞

Faith on Fire

Catholic Teens

*"I enjoy helping bring others closer to Christ.
Knowing that I have touched at least one person in
their journey of faith has helped me to grow faithfully."*

Katie Orlando, 18, high school
senior, Marietta, Georgia

∽

Twenty years ago, one would have been hard-pressed to find comprehensive youth ministry programs at a local Catholic parish. More often than not, "youth ministry" meant social activities such as dances or sports leagues grouped under the heading of Catholic Youth Organization (CYO). Today, however, the term enjoys a far broader definition. One cannot turn around without finding some type of dynamic youth ministry program.

Whether through a local parish youth ministry program or national programs such as Youth for the Third Millennium or Youth 2000, increasing numbers of teens are encountering Christ, embracing their Confirmation promises, re-igniting their faith, and connecting with the local and universal Church.

Catholic musician Kitty Cleveland remembers her involvement in CYO, growing up in New Orleans. "It was primarily social," says Cleveland. "It was very godless." Cleveland grew up an average Catholic in the pew; her faith was not particularly important to her until many years later.

"CYO was the first time that the Church really started looking at teens as individuals with different needs," recalls Barbara Anderson, program coordinator for the Secretariat for Family, Laity, Women, and Youth for the U.S. Conference of Catholic Bishops. "Today, youth ministry has expanded to include catechesis, social justice, and spiritual development."

Young and Catholic

Traditional youth ministry still ministers through programs and events for those young people who attend a local parish. The New Evangelization, however, also often involves going out to where the teens are.

Youth apostolates everywhere — Life Teen, Youth 2000, NET Ministries, Totus Tuus, Youth for the Third Millennium, the Diocese of Yakima's Reach Youth Ministry, and the Diocese of Fargo's Young Disciples Teams, to name a few — have seen a dramatic increase in their numbers over the past decade. Through such programs, teens are learning about their Faith and evangelizing at home and abroad.

In North Dakota, for example, Fargo's Young Disciples Teams recruit eighteen- to thirty-year-olds to host weeklong summer teen, family, and adult camps. For ten weeks at a time, the teams traverse the state, providing catechesis in North Dakota's Fargo and Bismarck dioceses and Minnesota's Crookston diocese. Through their witness, marked by a youthful, enthusiastic joy and the hope of faith, the teams challenge others to love Jesus Christ and to embrace the life of his family, the Church. Over the past three summers, the teams have shared the gospel with thousands of students, adults, and fellow teens.

One of the team members is twenty-one-year-old Anna Knier of Fargo. Currently a student at the University of Nebraska in Lincoln, Knier first encountered a Young Disciples Team after they had given a presentation in the basement of St. Mary's Cathedral. She has given up two summers to be a team member. She says she was initially attracted to join based on the experiences of a friend.

"I have a friend who was involved with Totus Tuus in Denver, Kansas, and Nebraska, and I assumed that this was similar," says Knier, who had worked as a counselor at a Catholic summer camp the previous two summers.

That's not to say that Knier didn't have her concerns.

"I was worried that I wouldn't see much fruit, and that would be discouraging to me," says Knier. Yet, she has found her time on the team fulfilling.

"I've become more selfless," she explains. "I'm also praying more — interceding for the children we meet, the parishes we're at, and fellow team members. Our efforts would be fruitless if we didn't take time for personal prayer."

While visiting a parish in Jamestown, North Dakota, Knier gave the youth a church tour. When she spoke about the tabernacle, one girl asked, "You mean Jesus is really in there?" When Knier replied yes, the girl prodded her friend and said, "Jesus is in there," and she stared at the tabernacle. "I was grinning on the inside," says Knier. "We're just planting seeds here."

Knier's time with the Young Disciples Team has also affected her career plans.

"I had been thinking that I might become a teacher," she says. "Now I'm thinking about getting a theology degree. After thirteen years of Catholic school, there's so much that I still don't know about my Faith, and I want to know more."

∽

Dead Theologians Society

Another innovative group that has seen tremendous growth is Newark, Ohio's Francis de Sales' Dead Theologians Society. Inspired by the 1989 film Dead Poets Society, the Dead Theologians are a fast-growing peer-to-peer teen movement.

Co-founded by Michael Barone and Eddy Cotter, the group has established more than fifty chapters around the world. The Dead Theologians combine prayer and evangelization for teens, largely by studying the lives of the saints.

Young and Catholic

"Imagine, these saints are all sitting there around God with favors to give us," explains Barone. "The Dead Theologians Society is bringing those individual graces to the aid of these kids through the intercession of each saint we study."

Barone says that they're reaching both the churched and unchurched: "We're reaching the black sheep, the druggie, the golfer, the goody-two-shoes, the jock. It's a very interesting family that God is building."

Michael Barone and Eddy Cotter co-founded the Dead Theologians Society, which combines prayer and evangelization for teens, chiefly through the study of the saints' lives.

Eighteen-year-old high school senior Jenny Lennon is among that family. She has participated in the Dead Theologians Society since her freshman year.

"Teens need someone to push us, to get us out of our cradle-Catholic comfort zone," says Lennon. "Hanging out with youth ministers who are living the Faith gave me the desire to know about God and to draw closer to Him. When we're given that kind of challenge, we change our hearts."

Another youth outreach program that's changing hearts is the St. Paul, Minnesota–based National Evangelization Team (NET) Ministries.

∞

NET Ministries

On the first Saturday of each month, approximately one thousand teens fill a converted gymnasium in West St. Paul for NET's lively Lifeline Mass. Joe Roueche, outreach coordinator for NET came up with the idea in 1995 as a way to make his organization more visible throughout the Twin Cities archdiocese. The early modest gatherings have become regular events with more than a thousand teens, often driving from as far away as Iowa, Wisconsin, and the Dakotas. NET is an international youth ministry, with offices in the United States, Canada, and Australia, that challenges young Catholics to love Christ and embrace the life of the Church.

As part of Lifeline, the teens listen to a Catholic speaker, sing, and celebrate Mass, including one Mass each year celebrated by Twin Cities' Archbishop Harry Flynn.

In addition to the monthly Mass, NET Ministries offers training in youth ministry and leads more than a thousand retreats annually across the United States, Canada, and Australia.

Roueche believes that World Youth Day has played a significant role in the success of Lifeline.

"The music might be what gets them here initially," Roueche says, "but the truth is what keeps them coming back. The Mass is always the pinnacle of the evening."

Far from being one-time mountaintop-like experiences, such activities impact the daily lives of these youths, and their future aspirations and plans.

Zack Hohenberg is a prime example. Following high school, Hohenberg decided to reach out to his peers in the United States, but first he had to set aside his love for basketball.

Four years ago, as a senior, Hohenberg led Farmington, New Mexico's Kirtland High School basketball team to a state title championship. Upon graduation, he hoped to find a college where he could continue playing, but the Holy Spirit had other plans. Instead, Hohenberg postponed college, giving a year of his life to evangelize Catholic youth through NET.

After attending one year at a community college in Albuquerque, Hohenberg hoped to move on to a university where he could play ball. Near the end of the school year, Zack's mother gave him information about NET Ministries.

"We live in a Mormon town," says Hohenberg, "and I was aware of the Mormon two-year missions. I wondered why the Catholic Church didn't have something similar."

Hohenberg at first set the application aside when he learned that NET teams did public speaking, performed skits, and hosted retreats.

"That was way out of my comfort zone," he admits.

A month later, he picked up the application again and applied.

"I wasn't doing anything with my life," says Hohenberg. "My mom had said that maybe I could work behind the scenes as part of the crew. That took some of the pressure off." Hohenberg interviewed. Three weeks later he was accepted.

He and eighty-four other teenagers went through extensive training before being sent off in teams of ten. Between September 2002 and May 2003, Hohenberg's team traveled throughout the Midwest and the Northeast, presenting as many as six youth retreats per week.

As a result, Hohenberg developed a deeper prayer life and a closer relationship with Christ.

"Prior to NET, I might have said a short prayer at night. Half the time I was falling asleep during it," says Hohenberg. "Now I realize that I need to pray every morning. It helps me get through the day."

He also met many interesting people along the way. Hohenberg recalled his meeting an eighth-grade student on one of the team's retreats.

"He prayed with us and told us he wanted to become a senator and use the Church's Faith as a tool as a senator. I thought that was awesome, and it gave me hope for the future of the Church."

∞

Teenage Trials

The teenage years are often years of searching and trying to find a place to fit in. In that search, many teens experiment with substance abuse and act out sexually. Statistics suggest that drug and alcohol abuse among teens has increased, and that sexual promiscuity and teen suicide are also on the rise. The answers that teens long for, the world cannot provide.

Amanda Smith learned that lesson the hard way. At the age of eighteen, Smith's Christian journey began while she was working as an au pair and vacationing with her employers in Rhode Island. Her only day off was Sunday. Normally, she went to the beach on her day off. One day, however, it was too early to go to the beach, so she drove to a quaint Episcopal church nearby. That morning, the church was celebrating a baptism.

"The service struck this powerful chord within me, and I recognized for the first time in my heart of hearts that Christ died just for me and that Baptism could make me new again," says Smith. "All at once, I was overcome by Christ's love for me and the heaviness of my past sin."

When Smith returned to her home in Connecticut, she started attending the nearest Episcopal church and asked to be baptized.

Back at home, however, surrounded by old friends, and much sin, she found living a pure life difficult.

"Sitting in the Episcopal church was so painful," she says. "I longed to be with young adults who, like me, wanted to live a life that was pleasing to God." At that point, Smith made the decision to leave the Episcopal church. She later joined a fundamentalist Baptist church. Still, she missed the tradition and liturgy that the Episcopal church offered, and the companionship of her peers, and her zeal and devotion to her faith were still immature. To fill the void, she was intimate with her boyfriend. Soon after she became pregnant.

Her boyfriend tried to convince her that abortion wasn't really a sin and told her that he would have nothing to do with her or the baby. In the end, Smith gave birth and placed the child up for adoption.

"Through all of this I became more disillusioned with the Christians around me," explains Smith, "so I switched churches again and began attending a Pentecostal church and an Assemblies of God college."

There she found hundreds of Christians her own age living in what she described as "a persistent web of sin and destruction."

"I decided that I could really no longer pretend to be a Christian when I was so frustrated by churches following the latest trends," she says.

In her early twenties, she met Giles, a self-proclaimed agnostic.

"Never had someone loved me so unselfishly and so generously," remarks Smith. The two got engaged and were married in an Episcopal church. She admits, however, that she never once acted like a Christian or even pretended to be one throughout their engagement and the first eighteen months of their marriage.

"When I finally understood that I must follow Christ again, I chose to attend the Episcopal church, where I had first fallen in love with our Lord," she recalls. "For all its beauty and tradition, though, I was angry that the biblical teachings and their articles of faith were largely ignored. I hated the church's lack of policy on homosexuality, and the ordination of women, and I prayed earnestly to be led to a church that had one set of rules and where pastors were accountable not only to God, but to a hierarchy."

After months of reading and prayer, she ultimately found what she was searching for — in the Catholic Church.

"I came to the conclusion that the Catholic Church was the Church that Christ had founded," she says. "Churches that had existed only a year — or four hundred years — couldn't offer the history that the Catholic Church had."

Today, Smith, thirty-two, owns a book-design business in Bradenton, Florida, where she lives with her husband and attends a Latin-rite Mass.

Of the Church she says, "I just got here. I'm not leaving. Ever!"

At the heart of the teenage search is not only the desire to belong to something larger than themselves, but also the opportunity to impact the larger culture through their service, sacrifice, and commitment. Life Teen is an example of one youth ministry program that works to provide such answers for teens.

∞

Teens Hunger to Be Loved

One of the largest organizations for expressing teen faith is Life Teen. It began, somewhat inconspicuously at St. Timothy's Catholic Community in Mesa, Arizona, in 1985. Today, more than a hundred thousand teens gather weekly for Life Teen Masses at nearly nine hundred parishes in virtually every state and twelve foreign countries.

The program began as a result of career indecision on the part of Catholic musician Tom Booth. Booth had graduated from the

Young and Catholic

University of Tucson in 1984 with a degree in music, but he wasn't sure what to do with his life.

"When I returned to Phoenix, I looked up Fr. Dale Fushek for spiritual direction," explains Booth, who had first met the priest many years before.

"Following Confession, Fr. Fushek asked me if I had health insurance. He said, 'I'm in need of a musician, and I've been thinking of offering you a job.' "

In April 1985, Booth began as music minister at St. Timothy's.

While there, he collaborated with Fr. Fushek and youth director Phil Baniewicz to create a dynamic youth program with a particular focus on the eucharistic celebration and music. The "Life Teen" program quickly grew from approximately four hundred people attending Sunday evening Mass weekly, to nearly two thousand.

"Is the Liturgy relevant to young people's lives?" asks Booth. "You need to be in relationship with young people in order to know that."

Booth explained that the culture of the young person used to change every five years. He believes that is no longer true.

"Between 1995 and 2000, there wasn't such a thing as a single youth culture. With influences such as MTV and the Internet, culture changes very quickly. There are now many subcultures with teens," Booth says.

Yet, while teen culture might change daily, the desires of the young remain the same.

"They hunger and thirst to be loved, to be valued, and to be told the truth," says Booth.

Teens involved with the group agree.

Without Life Teen, eighteen-year-old Katie Orlando doubts whether she would have ever gotten involved in her Faith.

"We went to church every Sunday, but it was just routine," she explains. "Life Teen has helped my faith to become my lifestyle," says Orlando, from Marietta, Georgia.

She first became involved in the organization four years ago because her brother had been involved and had attended World Youth Day in Rome.

Orlando's experiences, through weekly Life Teen Masses and Life Night presentations to her peers on topics including peer pressure and substance abuse, have helped her to make her faith a part of her everyday life. They have also spurred her on to greater involvement with her parish, her diocese, and other outreach work.

Two summers ago, Orlando traveled with other teens from her parish, St. Ann's Catholic Church, on a weeklong mission trip to Mustard Seed community in Kingston, Jamaica. There, she spent several days building and repairing homes, shoveling compost, bringing garbage to the local dump, and playing with the children.

"The children at Mustard Seed were very disabled," explains Orlando. "My experience with them taught me how to see the heart and soul of each child, how to look past their disabilities, and how to love them unconditionally."

In 2002 Orlando joined other Life Teen members in attending World Youth Day in Toronto. She says the experience left her speechless.

"Hearing the Holy Father speak about his love for us and the Church brought tears to my eyes," says Orlando. He inspired me to be proud to stand up in the midst of controversy and say that I love being Catholic. It's who I am."

Later that year, she did something she never would have done even a year before. She led an archdiocesan retreat on Christ titled "Who is this man?" for forty of her peers.

"I enjoyed being involved and helping bring others closer to Christ," says Orlando. "Knowing that I have touched at least one person in their journey of faith has helped me to grow faithfully."

Before Life Teen, Orlando explains that she was very down on herself.

"I didn't like who I was," she says.

But her involvement in the apostolate has changed her.

"Life Teen has taught me to see myself as Christ sees me, and how to see that in other people."

∞

Youth for the Third Millennium

Another thriving youth apostolate is Youth for the Third Millennium, based in Bethesda, Maryland. In 2001 and 2002 alone, the organization held more than ninety national and international missions, drawing about a thousand youth participants. In an effort that is part evangelization and part humanitarian aid, Youth for the Third Millennium participants spend their spring break not on the beach, but sharing their faith and carrying out humanitarian work: visiting orphans and the elderly and helping mission coordinators on projects in urban areas in the United States and Latin America. Youth for the Third Millennium is active in the Atlanta, Baton Rouge, Chicago, Dallas, Detroit, New York, Sacramento, St. Louis, and Toronto dioceses.

"Our apostolate draws young people who have a spiritual calling to share their faith with others," says Paul Bernetsky, executive director of Youth for the Third Millennium. "The number of local mission coordinators has grown dramatically in the past year alone."

Since its inception in 1995, more than four thousand youth have participated in the organization's missions, visiting more than two hundred thousand homes. One of the participants was Atlanta teenager Lindsay Di Rito.

In April 2003, Di Rito journeyed to Mexico with Youth for the Third Millennium to perform missionary work. Prior to her ten-day mission experience, the Atlanta sixteen-year-old was a lot like most teenagers. She wasn't active in her parish. She was frequently grouchy with the other members of her family. She loved to shop and travel.

That's how Lindsay's mother convinced her to participate in a Youth for the Third Millennium MegaMission to Mexico.

"When my mom asked if I wanted to go to Mexico, I wanted to go just to travel to Mexico," admits Di Rito.

Upon arriving, Di Rito wanted to return home. It wasn't what she expected. She didn't know many of the other teens, and she was dismayed by the grim conditions: "When I got there, I looked around and said, 'Okay, can we go now? I'm done.' "

By the second day, however, Di Rito's heart was changed. The daily routine had helped her bond with her peers and recognize the opportunity to make a difference.

Waking at seven each morning, the group of fourteen girls would "shower" using baby wipes, have a breakfast of *zucaritas* (frosted flakes), and then walk four miles to attend Mass in the mountain town of La Cima, four hours north of Mexico City.

After Mass the girls broke up into three groups to evangelize the towns of Huistongo, Xazylacacuco, and La Cima. As one of only three teens who knew Spanish, Di Rito served as the translator for her group.

"We would go door to door inviting the people to the sacraments, to activities, and to talks that we held at the church each day," explains Di Rito.

She was impressed by the generosity of the people.

"They would have holes in their clothing and ripped shoes, and yet when we knocked on their doors, they would invite us in and offer us food, or candy or soda," she explains. "Anything they had they would give you."

She recalls inviting one woman to Confession.

"She told us that she could not go because she had a bad leg and her hands hurt," explains Di Rito. "We asked her if she would go if we were able to get the man across the street to drive her, and she agreed."

After the man across the street agreed to drive her to church, the girls went back to the woman's house. "When we got there, the woman was already cleaned up and all dressed up for church. It was very cute," says Di Rito.

The experience was a real eye-opener for her.

"I thought I would be teaching them, but they taught me so much more," says Di Rito. "These people don't have clothes or money or cars, yet everyone there is so happy. When I came back, I realized how none of these things really matter. The only thing they have is God. The experience really deepened my faith."

Di Rito says that she had been transformed by her experience.

"I'm spending more time with my family and am nicer to them," says Di Rito. "I'm also trying to be less materialistic."

In addition, Di Rito's experience led to a stronger spiritual life. She became a member of the lay movement Regnum Christi, deepened her prayer life, and attended her first silent retreat.

"The retreat taught me what I had learned from Mexico, but helped to explain everything," Di Rito says.

As a senior, Di Rito is uncertain as to what her plans will be after high school. Yet her Mexico mission trip left a lasting impression on her.

"Now I'm considering becoming a translator," she concludes.

At home or abroad, nearly all teens share a love for music. Music speaks a universal language that transcends ethnic barriers. As such, it is a tool that is used by many Catholic musicians to reach teens and to teach the Faith. It's always a major element at teen gatherings and conferences, including World Youth Day. It's impossible to speak about teens without mentioning music. For many teens, contemporary Catholic and Christian music has become their entry point into the Church.

∞

Music as a Means of Evangelization

Contemporary Catholic musicians and bands aimed primarily at youth are on the rise. Several years ago, sales by record distributors such as Heartbeat Records were predominantly oriented to the traditional/liturgical marketplace with only one or two artists catering to youth and young-adult listeners. Today Heartbeat distributes more than fifty artists with recordings for youth.

That increase is notable not only in the United States, but also in Europe and Latin America, where Catholic recording artists attend music festivals nearly every month. One of the largest, the Song of Songs Festival, is held in Poland annually at the end of June.

"I feel this increase is mostly due to the Holy Father's love and attention to the youth and the increase in Catholic television programs oriented to youth," says Susan Stein, CEO of Donnellson, Iowa–based Heartbeat Records. Heartbeat was the first company to embrace contemporary Catholic music nearly nineteen years ago, originally using popular Irish singer Dana.

Catholic recording artists recognize that the young-adult market is one that cannot be ignored, and they are providing an alternative. With help from distributors such as Heartbeat Records and Troubadour for the Lord, they are filling a need.

Young and Catholic

Unity Award–winning Catholic musician Greg Walton views his contemporary Catholic rock music as a ministry. "When I was a teenager, my sister got involved in the occult and drugs," explains Walton. "My ministry is motivated by her experience."

When he's not teaching theology full-time at Fr. Ryan High School in Nashville, Tennessee, Walton performs about fifty concerts per year, most of them for youth.

"I do a lot of youth camps, Confirmation retreats, diocesan youth rallies, and parish concerts," says Walton. "Teens are in such a fragile state regarding holiness. They are going the world's way. God's heart pours out to young people. Through my music I try to encourage them to plug into Christ, the Church, and its teachings."

Daniel diSilva, lead singer and songwriter for the Dallas-based Catholic funk band Crispin, warns about the dark side of music.

"The music industry has a huge back door that leads directly to Hell," says diSilva, who performs at some 175 concerts per year. "Music is very powerful. It's easy to get sucked into all kinds of evil things. The musician on stage worships the fan, and vice versa."

Daniel diSilva is the lead singer and songwriter for the Catholic band Crispin.

In contrast, as an illustration of the positive power of music, Walton recalls an encounter with one teenage girl.

"My wife and I had played a concert and spoken about abstinence and my conversion," says Walton. "A year later, we went back with my band to the same location. While there, a girl told me, 'I was at the first talk that you gave. I'm a cocaine addict. I've been clean for six months and have been trying to clean up. I wanted to thank you.' That is the crux of what my music is about."

The challenge for the industry is how to compete and market the music.

"Youth don't often go into Catholic bookstores, so how do we reach them?" asks Walton. "It's a catch-22. Radio stations don't want to play you unless you're in the stores, and stores don't want to stock you if you're not on the radio."

One band that has been able to surmount that hurdle is the Nashville-based Celtic rock band Ceili Rain. Ceili Rain has succeeded in crossing over from Catholic to Contemporary Christian distributors. Their records are carried in stores such as Borders and Tower Records.

Like Walton, Ceili Rain performs many diocesan youth rallies. The band has also performed at the National Catholic Youth Convention and World Youth Day in both Rome and Toronto.

Ceili Rain differs from some of the other bands in that they do not actively proselytize. "They bring us in when the youth just want to rock. Yet the adults want them to do it in a way that isn't harmful," explains lead singer Bob Halligan, Jr. "In the past, they've had dances with mainstream music with questionable content. The kids hear enough of that. They need to hear something different. We bring in rock music that's coming from a wholesome place."

Halligan believes that the contemporary Christian music has had a positive impact on Catholic music for teens.

"I get the feeling that the Catholics and Evangelical Protestants are infecting each other more than we all realize," says Halligan. "The increased enthusiasm among Catholic youth for matters of faith, and the increased numbers of Catholic youth active in youth groups and youth rallies is somewhat attributable to seeing their friends attend contemporary Christian music concerts. I really believe that there are ways in which the two sides can complete each other."

DiSilva warns of attempts to transform Catholic contemporary music into Protestant Contemporary Christian or praise and worship music. While he's encouraged to see the rise of contemporary Catholic musicians, he doesn't see them duplicating the success of Protestants, for one very good reason.

"We'll never get as excited about our music and prayer as the Protestants do, because we have the Eucharist," explains diSilva. "We have the same kind of excitement for the Eucharist. Catholic music points us toward that. If Catholics ever get as excited about praise and worship music as the Protestants do, then we will have lost something. Good Catholic music should point people to the Eucharist, and there, before Christ, the music is going to be silence itself."

∽

Recognizing the Truths of the Faith

Not only do young faithful Catholics have a unique passion for their Faith, but they also possess a healthy desire to learn more — a desire that is often absent in the previous generation. Those who embrace the Faith demonstrate a remarkable ability to articulate that love.

When the West Chester, Pennsylvania–based publisher Ascension Press conducted its first annual National Catholic Education youth essay contest (the topic, "Why I Love Being Catholic") in November 2001, it expected no more than three hundred essays. But in the end, young people from the United States, Canada, and Europe submitted more than two thousand responses.

Among the essays, the Eucharist figured largely. Fifteen of the top twenty finalists wrote of their appreciation of the Eucharist in the life of the Church.

"I used to feel lonely during Holy Communion, because everybody else was able to accept the Body and Blood of Jesus Christ and I couldn't," wrote America Yamaguchi, a fifth-grade homeschool student from Belmont, California.

Yamaguchi's family was Buddhist. At the age of nine, her mother converted to the Catholic Church. Yamaguchi was baptized as a Catholic at Easter 2002.

Another third-place winner, Erin Doyle, of Alto, Michigan, compared her faith to a precious treasure in her poem, "The Treasure Box":

> In the heart of the Treasure Box,
> you will find Jesus,
> truly present in the Eucharist,
> > Body,
> > Blood,
> > Soul, and
> > Divinity.
> There He has been since the Church began,
> His Presence is the reason why I truly
> > am proud of my Treasure,
> Without it, the Church would not be as strong.
> In the Eucharist,
> Christ fulfilled His promise to be with us
> > and guide us always.

Bethany Stokman, of Crosby, Minnesota, was awarded the grand prize in the fifth-through-eighth-grade category. She wrote of her family's departure from the Catholic Church when she was five years old, in part because her parents did not believe in the Eucharist. She also wrote of their eventual return.

"Even though we don't always feel God's presence in the Eucharist or see it, we believe and know in our hearts that it is true," wrote Stokman.

She cited it as the reason she loves being Catholic.

"I am being fed . . . fed from the banquet of Heaven!" she wrote.

Several students wrote of their appreciation for the Church's authority.

"I am thankful to be a Catholic because the Catholic Church has the authority to teach, to sanctify, and to rule," wrote senior grand-prize-winning student Stephen Tillotson from Petoskey, Michigan. "Although many dissidents resent the authority of the Church, it is necessary for her well being," wrote Tillotson. "An illustration of this is the numerous and diverse Protestant churches. The reason for the vast number of them is the fact that they have rejected the authority of the Church. In doing so, they have placed each man in the position of pope. Therefore, there is no one to explain the truths of religion and to render moral judgments for the Protestant who seeks the truth. Instead he must decide for himself what he will believe."

"We have the Magisterium, the authority, to guide us through hard times and questionable moments," wrote sixth-grade student Mary Anderson of Alpine, California. "This is probably one of the greatest things we have, for Jesus gave us spiritual leaders through Peter, our first pope, when He said, 'And so I say to you, you are Peter, and upon this Rock I will build my Church.' "

Although some young people have a clear understanding of their Faith at an early age, for many others that clarity comes later. The mission trips and evangelization efforts might, at first glance, appear to be singular events for youth. Yet, such experiences in youth groups often provide the early formation for a lifelong devotion to Christ and His Church. Their continued involvement can be witnessed on university campuses and beyond.

∞

Does This Hold Water?

Christ on Campus

*"I'm hoping to go to a very good, 'traditional'
Catholic university where a pro-life, practicing Catholic
is not treated like an outcast. As for the future,
I'm open to what God wants me to do with my life."*

Tom Wills, 17, high school senior, Burke, Virginia

❦

Increasing numbers of university students are not only receiving an education while at college; they are also embracing the Faith. The evidence can be seen at Catholic and non-Catholic schools alike. Kelly Heinz attended Michigan's Hillsdale College to earn a degree. But in the end, she received far more than a piece of paper. Her time at Hillsdale also led her to the Catholic Church.

"I grew up in a non-Christian home," says Heinz, who graduated in 2002 with a degree in English. "Growing up, occasionally I would attend the Catholic Church with friends. I always liked the reverence that I found in the Catholic Church."

In what Heinz referred to as a "holy coincidence," her roommates during her freshman and sophomore year were Catholic. Interested in Christianity, Heinz made an intense study of the various denominations. Ultimately, a study of the Gospel of John led her to embrace Catholicism.

"When Christ said, 'This is my body. . . . This is my blood,' He really meant it," says Heinz. "You don't find that anywhere else nearly as seriously as in the Catholic Church."

Following a yearlong process through the Rite of Christian Initiation for Adults (RCIA) at St. Anthony's Catholic Church in Hillsdale, Heinz came into the Church at Easter 2002.

"Students are looking for stability," says Melinda Ziegler, pastoral administrator and RCIA director at St. Anthony's. "They have been with their parents for eighteen years and are now saying, 'I have to see if this holds water.' "

Ziegler has worked on the RCIA team for the past decade. While in the past she has had one or two students from the college in RCIA, recent years have seen an increase. In 2003, one-sixth of her class of thirty was made up of college students from nearby Hillsdale.

This trend is evident on other campuses as well.

One of the most popular college RCIA programs in the country is at St. Mary's Student Center at Texas A&M. Over the past six years, the program there has seen between eighty and a hundred young adults enter the Church each year.

RCIA director Martha Tonn attributes the increase to a variety of factors.

"We have a strong emphasis on the sacraments," says Tonn. "Nearly two hundred college students attend Mass daily, and the sacrament of Reconciliation is offered twice during the week to accommodate students. We have eucharistic adoration at various times each day."

"Another reason for the increase," explains the center's pastor, Fr. Michael Sis, "is the fact that our students are coming from more complete programs of youth ministry in their home parishes. They seem to be coming to college with much better Catholic formation than they did ten or fifteen years ago."

There's also the social aspect.

Understanding the need for hospitality and fellowship, St. Mary's hosts Bible studies, praise and worship groups, and retreats nearly every night of the week.

"I have been amazed at how many people tell me that they come to RCIA because a friend invited them to Mass," says Tonn. "They felt invited and welcomed, and so they just kept coming."

Another college ministry program that has tried to capitalize on both socialization and evangelization is the apostolate Fellowship of Catholic University Students (FOCUS), based in Greeley, Colorado. The program has seen a great number of conversions.

∽

The Faith in Focus

FOCUS operates on eighteen college campuses in ten states. With the permission of the local bishop, and in collaboration with existing campus ministry programs, FOCUS staff members train students to evangelize and invite others into campus ministry. The program is modeled after popular nondenominational campus ministries such as InterVarsity Christian Fellowship and Campus Crusade for Christ, which tend to pull students away from the Catholic Church.

The success of FOCUS is due, in part, to what founder Curtis Martin describes as "spiritual multiplication."

"We ask student leaders to invest in three people, and they, in turn, ask those three to invest in three more. By doing the math of spiritual multiplication, we can reach the world for Christ in our lifetime," explains Martin.

FOCUS's director of marketing and public relations, Libby Ariniello, says that the organization does not quantify conversions to Christ. However, she says that great numbers of students have had what she described as a "lights-on experience" through FOCUS, many even in the first few months after the organization has started on a campus.

"For some, that means having a powerful experience of Christ in the Eucharist," says Ariniello. "For others, it means joining a Bible study, returning to regular Sunday Mass, or just making something that they have had all along their own."

Ariniello estimates that some fifteen hundred students are somehow involved in FOCUS nationwide. In January 2003, the organization's leadership conference drew more than 620 students from fifty schools across the country.

Nicole Beran, campus director of FOCUS at the University of Illinois at Champaign-Urbana, attributes her conversion, in part, to her involvement with FOCUS at the University of Nebraska. Although she grew up Catholic, she admits that she hadn't internalized her faith.

"Sunday Mass was the extent of my Catholic lifestyle," says Beran.

During her senior year, Beran encountered FOCUS at the campus student union.

"I walked past the FOCUS sign and decided, 'Why not see what this is all about,' " she says. Relatively new on campus, Beran heard through word of mouth that FOCUS provided a time for students to gather together to talk about their Catholic Faith and have fellowship with one another. Beran signed up for a Bible study.

"I couldn't believe the things I heard in that study," recalls Beran. "I remember hearing about God being our loving Father, that He wants to bring us happiness, that He has a plan for our lives, and that His Son, Jesus, will return. I had been searching for something like this for a long time, so when I heard it, it resonated with me, and I couldn't get enough."

Eventually, Beran felt she was called to serve FOCUS as a staff member. She has served at the University of Illinois for three years. She sees college students struggling with the same search that she experienced.

"College students are constantly being told that success in leadership is about getting more money, building the best resume, finding the best jobs, being able to buy a huge home. It's all about more and more and more," says Beran. "Deep down, though, they realize where their true home is, and they are attracted to fellow students who are living the Christian life."

Beran estimates that there are more than a hundred students active in FOCUS at the University of Illinois. FOCUS groups are leading seventeen Bible studies, ten of which are student-run.

FOCUS has had success on Catholic campuses as well. As evidence, Ariniello cites Benedictine College in Atchison, Kansas.

"Prior to FOCUS's presence on campus, Fr. Meinrad Miller, OSB, director of campus ministry at Benedictine College, told us that only five to ten students were coming to daily Mass. Today, they are seeing as many as two hundred students per day," says Ariniello. "Fr. Miller believes that FOCUS's role on campus has played a part in the increased interest."

At Benedictine College, more than two hundred students attend daily Mass, and an equal number participate in on-campus Bible studies; some three hundred skip a meal each week and donate the food to the poor; and in the past year alone the college has seen nine students go on to a religious vocation.

That Catholicism extends to Benedictine's residence halls.

"All resident directors study the virtues, *Ex Corde Ecclesiae*, the Rule of St. Benedict, the Pope's *Theology of the Body*, and the documents on the dignity of the human person and the vocation of women," says Fr. Brendan Rolling, director of residence life and assistant dean of students.

"We explain the rationale behind the policies at Benedictine," explains Fr. Rolling. "Our visitation policy, for example, doesn't just say that you can't visit someone of the opposite sex at a certain time. Our hope is that deep friendships will form while students are on campus and that students discover their vocations through those friendships. The best way for those relationships to be sustained and to grow is through chaste relationships."

Fr. Rolling admits that he hears more confessions and does more spiritual direction than he deals with discipline problems. "We hear confessions at nine p.m., a half hour before Mass, but the demand from students was so high that we started doing confessions again after Mass. There are times when we don't leave chapel until one in the morning."

Issues with student discipline have dropped considerably since. "It's amazing what we've seen happen on campus," Fr. Rolling adds.

Still, Benedictine deals with the normal problems facing every college campus. "We still have all the normal problems," says Fr. Rolling, "but students are coming to terms with them through the sacraments." Fr. Rolling is no stranger to the power of the Faith. He discerned his vocation, in part, from attending World Youth Day in Denver.

"The number of spontaneous ministries that are arising from students is just exploding," says Fr. Rolling. "There is a group of thirty students who have a Christian music ministry to juvenile delinquents in the community. In addition to small-group Bible studies, there are groups who pray the Daily Office together prior to bedtime and others who go on hiking trips, but ask to have Mass included as part of it."

Senior Nathan Stanley, from Liberty, Missouri, says that the school's Catholic character has influenced not only his spiritual life, but also his career aspirations. Stanley has worked in the president's office and hopes to pursue a career in Catholic higher-education administration.

"The professors at Benedictine teach with the Church," says Stanley. "They quote the Holy Father. You can tell they are with the Church's teachings full-throttle."

Secular colleges and universities aren't often the places where one expects to find great faith. Yet, the Brotherhood of Hope is having extraordinary success reaching students who have fallen away from their Faith on three such campuses.

∞

Brotherhood of Hope

Founded in 1980 by Fr. Philip Merdinger and four other men, the Brotherhood of Hope is a Boston-based canonically recognized Catholic community of brothers and priests serving young adults, carrying out a men's ministry, teaching catechesis, and leading campus-based retreats. The Brotherhood works in campus ministry at Boston University, the University of Massachusetts at Lowell, and Florida State University. Through their Eucharist-centered retreats, their Bible studies, and their committed presence on campus, the community's twenty brothers and priests are reaching many lapsed and uncommitted Catholic students.

Christine Songy was first impressed by the dedication of the Brotherhood of Hope while a junior at Boston University. On a fall retreat, Fr. Paul Helfrich agreed to hear the college student's confessions. Although Fr. Helfrich had invited a second priest to help, the second priest had to leave after only an hour. Fr. Helfrich, on the other hand, remained for six hours until every student had had a chance to receive the sacrament of Reconciliation.

"He was up until two a.m. That made an impact on me," says Songy, who graduated as valedictorian of her undergraduate class and now works as a physical therapist in Norfolk, Virginia. "Here was a man who was devoted to helping us grow closer to God. It was very Christlike."

That dedication manifests itself in sometimes unconventional ways on the various campuses where the Brotherhood operates.

Young and Catholic

At the University of Massachusetts–Lowell, Br. Ken Apuzzo, Jr. leads a weekly Bible study with the school's Division 1 hockey team. Half the team attends the study every Wednesday night at the ice arena.

Br. Patrick Reilly, who holds a black belt in karate, teaches self-defense classes in the residence halls, and on moving day, the brothers help students move into the dormitories.

"This allows the students to see that the brothers are normal guys," says Br. Apuzzo. "That way, when you later invite them to a larger event such as Mass or a retreat, they come. Often it's only because of our personal relationship with them that they will come."

Come, they do. At the University of Massachusetts–Lowell, the attendance at Mass and other ministry events has clearly increased. Songy witnessed a similar expansion at Boston University after the Brotherhood arrived there four years ago.

"Eucharistic adoration went from once a semester, to once a month, to every other week, to every week," she says. "Praise and worship night went from every other week to weekly."

As a result of the students' now evangelizing their own peers, the number of Boston University students attending retreats has more than quadrupled. Moreover, the Newman Center house is now too small for some of their events and programs.

The growth at Florida State University is even more impressive, especially given that Catholics are a minority in North Florida.

There, nearly sixteen hundred students attend Mass weekly, and roughly 150 attend a weekly Wednesday-evening gathering. Retreats on campus often draw more than two hundred students, with another hundred on a waiting list.

"I welcomed the Brotherhood of Hope into my diocese and assigned them to the campus ministry at Florida State University," says former Pensacola-Tallahassee Bishop John M. Smith, who now serves the Diocese of Trenton. "I was pleased by their work with college students and was impressed by their zeal and dedication." Still, it isn't always easy reaching students. Observing student life, Br. Apuzzo says he sees a "disconnect" taking place between God and the Church.

"Modern individualism has really influenced the spiritual life of our students," says Br. Apuzzo. "They will say, 'I believe in God, but I don't feel like I have to go to church.' They often do not have a clearly articulated concern against the Church. It's mostly ignorance."

The brothers work to change that. This often begins by building relationships and inviting students to smaller events, such as a social or sporting event or praise and worship night. The brothers spend much of their time finding nonthreatening ways to enter into the student culture.

"We can often get them on a retreat before we can get them to Mass," adds Br. Apuzzo. "They come to see one another, but Mass is always where we are headed. It is the spiritual high point."

Boston University alumnus Songy agrees.

"I've seen the Brotherhood pull in so many kids who would never be caught dead at a religious function," says Songy.

Others have observed what they describe as a real spiritual transformation take place among students.

"Prior to the brothers' coming, campus ministry was primarily social. Now the intensity of the spirituality is palpable," says Thomas Neal, a religion teacher at John Paul II High School in Tallahassee who first came to know the Brotherhood after their arrival at Florida State in 1994. "Lukewarm students become passionate about their faith."

Neal adds that he has seen the work of the Brotherhood produce many "rock-solid marriages" and religious vocations. In the fall of 2004, five men entered the Pensacola-Tallahassee diocesan seminary. Four of them came through the Brotherhood's ministry. During the 2003-2004 school year, fifteen young women on campus were actively discerning religious life.

In addition to the retreats that the Brotherhood host on campus each semester, they have offered "Hope on Campus" retreats at other colleges, such as the University of Maryland, Williams College, and the Air Force Academy in Colorado Springs.

Brother Apuzzo explains that the retreats are often a time of tremendous conversion.

"On Friday night we introduce students to eucharistic adoration and explain why the Eucharist is so central to Catholic life," says Brother Apuzzo. "At first, some are fearful. They've never seen it before."

But by Sunday the brothers often witness a transformation.

"It's very uplifting to watch," adds Br. Apuzzo. "By Sunday, you can see the reverence in their body language and in the way they receive Communion. They recognize that they are receiving the real life of Jesus."

"What's unique about the brothers are the consistently positive fruits that come from them and the effects they have on people," says Neal. "They affect a lot of people even though their ministry is campus-focused. They don't just affect the students, but also the homeless population, the business community, and family life."

∞

The Rise of the Catholic Liberal-Arts College
The increasing secularization of many of America's oldest and most prominent Catholic colleges and universities has made many such Catholic institutions virtually indistinguishable from their

secular counterparts. In fact, at a majority of the country's 235 Catholic colleges and universities, Catholic parents and students are unable to learn whether the theology faculty have applied for or received the Church's *mandatum* — an agreement between the individual theologian and the local bishop that affirms that the theologian will teach in concert with the teachings of the Church.

In response to this growing secularization, marked by pro-abortion commencement speakers, student groups that advocate for homosexual relationships, the removal of crucifixes from classroom walls, and a lack of Catholic professors on campus, the past three decades have witnessed a renewal of Catholic higher education through the rise of smaller Catholic liberal-arts colleges that pride themselves on their fidelity to the Church.

If college campuses are the place where the Faith can have the largest impact upon the future of society, then the future of the New Evangelization is being played out at places such as Aquinas College in Nashville, Tennessee; Ave Maria University in Naples, Florida; Benedictine College in Atchison, Kansas; Christendom College in Front Royal, Virginia; Corpus Christi College in Corpus Christi, Texas; De Sales University in Center Valley, Pennsylvania; Franciscan University of Steubenville in Steubenville, Ohio; Washington D.C.'s John Paul II Institute for Marriage and Family; Thomas Aquinas College in Santa Paula, California; and the University of Dallas. In the spring of 2004, plans were announced for at least two additional new Catholic colleges — Wyoming Catholic College and San Diego's New Catholic College.

Students at Thomas Aquinas College are praying twice a week outside an abortion business. At Benedictine College a large number of students forgo their lunch once a week and donate the food and money to the local soup kitchen. At Franciscan University of Steubenville, female upperclassmen stage a modesty fashion show for incoming students and pepper the campus with "WWMW" stickers, reminding students "What would Mary wear?" Such institutions are producing a vibrant new generation of Catholic leaders.

∞

California's Jewel

One of Catholic higher education's jewels is found on the West Coast: Thomas Aquinas College, near Santa Paula, California.

Bordering the Los Padres National Forest, Thomas Aquinas College's campus is set on a 131-acre former ranch between Santa Paula and Ojai, California. The college offers a truly unique undergraduate experience — offering a classical Great Books liberal education that remains true to the teachings of the Catholic Church. The college provides no lectures or textbooks, has no majors, and offers no electives. All classes are conducted using only the Socratic method of discussion. All students take the same courses — reading only the original writings of those authors whose thoughts helped shape Western Civilization, including Augustine, Aquinas, Plato, Cicero, Descartes, Aristotle, Shakespeare, Euclid, and Einstein.

The college began as an idea, first expressed in 1969.

American Catholics are becoming increasingly aware of the growing tendency of Catholic colleges to secularize themselves — that is, to loosen their connection with the teaching Church and to diminish deliberately their Catholic character. Catholic parents in particular are becoming alarmed at the effects that this secularization has or threatens to have on the intellectual and moral formation of their children. The colleges themselves display a growing inability to define themselves in such a way as to justify their continued existence as Catholic institutions.

So opens the founding document of the college, "A Proposal for the Fulfillment of Catholic Liberal Education," which has since become known simply as the "Blue Book."

Instead of lectures, all classes at Thomas Aquinas College use the Socratic method of discussion about the works of authors whose thoughts helped shape Western civilization.

Written by Dr. Ronald McArthur, Marc Berquist, and John Neumayr, the document sought to describe the crisis in modern Catholic education and to affirm that faith can illumine understanding.

When it opened its doors in September 1971, the college attracted thirty-three students. Class size has doubled since then, and 2003's graduating class was the largest in the school's history — seventy-seven students from the U.S., Kenya, and China.

Aside from the campus, little has changed in the college's thirty-two years. All students take a common curriculum — four years of theology, philosophy, math, science, and literature, two years of Latin, and one year of music theory.

"The goal of the program isn't necessarily to get a job; it is to form the mind so you can lead a human life," says Glen Coughlin, college dean. "We're devoted to doing one thing and doing it well. It is only a beginning, but it has great depth."

The school is Catholic to the core. All the Catholic professors — or "tutors," as they're known — have taken the Oath of Fidelity to the Magisterium. A priest resides in its largest men's residence hall. Mass is offered three times a day. Religious artwork and statues are tastefully appointed. The buildings bear the names of the Church's saints, and a crucifix adorns every classroom wall.

However, the Catholicism of the college is evident in far more than the campus's physical surroundings. It is also evident in the seriousness with which the students embrace their studies and prayer life, and in the humility of its tutors.

The rich spiritual life — Mass, the Rosary, the Chaplet of Divine Mercy, the opening of each class with prayer, and other devotions — are not imposed by the administration. Rather, they are practices requested by the students, and they highlight the impact of the Church's intellectual life on the life of the average student.

Students' commitment to their faith manifests itself in a variety of ways, from intentional prayer to Christian action. In the fall of 2003, a group of students were effective in helping to bring about the closure of Family Planning Associates, a local abortion business. The closing came after six years of twice-weekly prayer at the clinic. The prayer group had been started by nineteen-year-old Angela Baird of Spokane, Washington, in 1997.

According to Angela's mother, Peggy, Angela began pro-life sidewalk counseling work on her own initiative in the ninth grade.

Altar servers lead a formal procession for baccalaureate Mass through a campus archway at Thomas Aquinas College.

"The life issues were something we had discussed as a family," explains Peggy, "and Angela had that interest. She kept pushing, as fourteen-year-olds will."

Angela marched in rallies in Spokane, and eventually went through training to be a sidewalk counselor. She often did sidewalk counseling at Planned Parenthood.

"Later in high school, she attempted to get friends to go with her," says her mother. "She was disappointed that people wouldn't go down with her. She was also disappointed that there wasn't a group at Thomas Aquinas College."

Angela organized a small group of Thomas Aquinas College students to pray in front of Family Planning Associates' Ventura office every Thursday, a day when abortions were performed. On the afternoon of Angela's death, nearly a hundred students gathered to pray fifteen decades of the Rosary and the chaplet of Divine Mercy in front of the office.

In her sophomore year, Baird was killed in a tragic hiking accident. She was with a group of seven other students on a hiking trail in Los Padres National Forest, located behind the campus, when she lost her footing on an overhang and fell sixty feet onto the rocks below.

Her friend Jon Daly, then a junior, quickly went to aid her. He placed a rosary in her hand and prayed with her until the paramedics arrived three hours later.

"I asked her what she wanted to pray for," recalls Daly. "The first thing she said was to pray for aborted babies; then she said to pray for her dad and to her guardian angel."

In a letter to Angela's parents Daly wrote, "I will never forget that reply; her love for the unborn and the aborted is one of the most beautiful things about Angela's life."

Much to students' surprise, the abortion business closed exactly six years to the day after Baird's death.

Thomas Aquinas College students volunteer weekly for prayer and sidewalk counseling in front of an abortion clinic in nearby Ventura.

Student-initiated efforts, such as Baird's, are an inspiration to both students and staff at the college.

"Students faithfully passed down this ministry to the unborn — and the story of the young woman who started it — from year to year," says Norbertine Fr. Michael Perea, the college chaplain. To see this kind of faith in our students is a real inspiration for all of us."

∽

Aquinas's Students

"My brother, who graduated in 1993, has always been able to outsmart me," says Judith Stachyra, a 2002 graduate from Essex, Illinois. "I came to Thomas Aquinas because I wanted my thinking to be clear. It was the only college to which I applied. It has been everything I had hoped for, and more."

Veronica Rioux, a junior from Lewiston, Maine, says that she enjoys being with others of like mind.

"The college is not only a good teacher of virtue; it is an encouragement to see others succeed. It makes living out your faith easier," Rioux explains.

The college's statistics are impressive. Nearly fifty percent of the graduates go on to graduate school, and the *National Review College Guide* has named the school among the top fifty liberal-arts schools in America. *U.S. News and World Report* ranks it among the top hundred. Eleven percent of its alumni enter religious life. Two are now presidents of colleges. Others have become successful in the fields of law, medicine, teaching, and business.

Just one example of the caliber of the school's graduates is Pia de Solenni. A thirty-four-year-old native of Crescent City, California, de Solenni received her undergraduate degree from Thomas Aquinas College and her doctorate from the Pontifical University of the Holy Cross in Rome. In 2001, she received the Award of the Pontifical Academies for her dissertation analyzing feminist theories and developing an integral feminism in light of St. Thomas Aquinas's philosophy.

It was during her freshman year at Thomas Aquinas that she realized she wanted to pursue theology.

"When you see the unity of truth, you want to pursue the highest truth, which is theology," says de Solenni, who is on leave from her position as director of life and women's issues with the Family Research Council while pursuing a Bradley Fellowship at the University of Notre Dame.

De Solenni has had numerous encounters with the Holy Father, including receiving her award from him.

"I told him that an entire John Paul II generation thanks him and prays for him," she says.

Students at the more secularized Catholic schools are also working toward greater respect of their Catholic identity. One of the ways this is taking shape is through the rise of independent Catholic newspapers on such campuses.

∞

Independent Catholic
Newspapers on Campus

On a growing number of Catholic college campuses, efforts are under way to give faithful Catholic students a voice through the establishment of "alternative" Catholic newspapers. The effort is the work of the Catholic Campus Media Network, a project of the Cardinal Newman Society that was launched in 2002. In 2003, students could find such newspapers on at least seven of the nation's Catholic college campuses. The papers are providing faithful students a voice where there previously has not been one.

"At so many schools, there are faithful Catholics looking for an authentically Catholic voice on campus," says Kathryn Jean Lopez, editor of *National Review* Online and volunteer director of the project. "If the students have to be the ones to provide it, so be it." Lopez is a graduate of Catholic University of America.

The Cardinal Newman Society launched the network in an effort to help establish campus publications that provide news and commentary from a Catholic, traditional-values perspective. They were motivated to undertake the project after witnessing the success that newspapers such as Georgetown's *The Academy* and Boston College's *Crossroads* had demonstrated in presenting a Catholic viewpoint on those campuses.

"At many colleges and universities, campus publications focus primarily on general news and pay little attention to Catholic issues and perspectives," explains Patrick Reilly, president of the Cardinal Newman Society. "But the Network's members are dedicated to building a Christian campus culture."

Reilly points to the "crucifix campaign" at Georgetown University in 1997 as an example of how independent student publications can raise concerns and effect changes in university policies.

Six years ago, students at Georgetown formed the Georgetown University Committee for Crucifixes in the Classrooms, petitioning the administration to have crucifixes placed in the classrooms. That move set off a campus debate. Georgetown's independent newspaper *The Academy* successfully argued the case for crucifixes.

"I wasn't personally involved, but it was an effort we definitely supported," says Barry Schiffman, editor-in-chief of *The Academy*. In the end, Georgetown agreed to put up the crucifixes. "We were happy once it succeeded," adds Schiffman, a law student who has been working with the paper since his sophomore undergraduate year in 1998.

Young and Catholic

Alternative Catholic newspapers exist on six Catholic university campuses, including *Justice* at the University of Dallas, *Fenwick Review* at College of the Holy Cross, *The Gonzaga Witness* at Gonzaga University, *CUA World* at Catholic University, and *Villanova Times* at Villanova.

One of the newest is *Justice*, published at the University of Dallas.

"While the University of Dallas campus newspaper did an outstanding job reporting happenings on campus, there was no section devoted to issues of special interest to Catholic students," says editor Jason Van Dyke. In response, Van Dyke created *Justice*.

Van Dyke is no stranger to starting a newspaper. A former student at Michigan State University, Van Dyke started *The Spartan Spectator* after being dismissed from the university's *State News* staff for articles he wrote criticizing the campus's homosexual-rights movement. He later transferred to Dallas, and at Easter 2003 the former Southern Baptist entered the Church.

Van Dyke also created a handbook for students who want to start independent newspapers.

"The handbook will teach students how to do all those things necessary to start and maintain a successful Catholic newspaper on their campus without breaking the rules," he says.

Rules or no rules, the establishing of independent newspapers is not without its difficulties. In addition to university protocol, there is frequent turnover, and funding can be difficult to obtain.

Fr. Robert Friday describes two of the hurdles.

"Independent newspapers must go through the student activities office to obtain permission for distribution," says Fr. Friday, former vice president for student life at Catholic University of America. Explaining the turnover, Fr. Friday says, "Like many student organizations, newspapers come and go depending upon the student environment and leadership."

Additionally, because the newspapers are independent, they seldom receive funding from the university. Instead, they rely largely on alumni and advertising for support. Lopez says that she is most encouraged by the fact that the effort has been student-driven.

"For the most part, there has been no prodding involved," she says. "At places like Holy Cross, for instance, where the administration allows plays such as *The Vagina Monologues* the newspaper serves as an oasis."

"Catholic colleges rarely evangelize and catechize students, yet many young Catholics come to school unprepared for Theology 101," Reilly explains. "This is exactly what the Church needs: faithful Catholic students reaching out to their peers. Most Catholic colleges will welcome such a positive and exciting program."

To bolster their efforts, the network partnered with two nonprofits, the Intercollegiate Studies Institute and the Leadership Institute, to offer training and start-up grants for independent-newspaper editors.

"Conservative or traditional ideas have been maligned, silenced, or censored at ninety-eight percent of universities in America," says Rich Moha, spokesman for the Leadership Institute.

The Leadership Institute embarked on a project to start independent conservative political newspapers on college campuses in 1983. To date, they have helped to start at least seventy such publications.

Reilly pointed out that the Cardinal Newman Society is interested in supporting student publications of all political stripes, as long as they accurately present and embrace Catholic doctrine.

Young and Catholic

∞

Signs of Renewal

Organizations such as the Cardinal Newman Society and FOCUS are working for the renewal of Catholic higher education. So are individuals, such as corporate executive Donald D'Amour.

In an effort to acknowledge the work of institutions such as Thomas Aquinas and Benedictine College, Catholic Massachusetts' businessman Donald D'Amour — CEO of Big Y Foods, Inc. — and his wife, Michelle, established the $1.5 million *Fides et Ratio* Grant Competition in 2000. The grant, inspired by Pope John Paul II's 1998 encyclical letter, supports the pursuit of wisdom by nurturing both faith and reason.

"I had heard for years of people complaining about the preparedness of students and wondered what would happen if Catholic colleges tried to be a bit more aggressive in attracting particular students who could contribute to the mission of a Catholic liberal-arts education," explains D'Amour.

"The grant was also based upon my own experience of having visited several Catholic colleges with my five children and seeing how they presented their cases. I found that I wasn't all that successful. There was a glaring disconnect between what the schools proclaim their mission to be and their admission practices," says D'Amour. "I wondered what would happen if we encouraged Catholic colleges to incorporate their admission programs as part of their mission."

Through a competitive process involving sixteen invited institutions, the grant seeks to encourage and assist small Catholic liberal-arts colleges in enrolling and educating students who desire to understand their Faith as integral to their educational experience. Fourteen colleges participated in the application process in January 2000.

The grant committee included D'Amour as well as such notables as Cardinal Avery Dulles; Dr. John Agreso, former president of St. John's College in Santa Fe; Dr. Patrick Powers, executive director of the grant; Fr. James Schall; and Dr. Frederick Crosson. "One and a half million dollars would mean peanuts to a place like the University of Notre Dame," says D'Amour. "We had neither the resources nor the hubris to believe that we could affect larger institutions, so we invited sixteen smaller schools to participate."

In August 2002, the grant competition presented awards to the finalists, which included many of the rising stars in Catholic higher education: Benedictine College, DeSales University, Thomas Aquinas College, and Thomas More College.

"For Catholic liberal-arts colleges to survive, it's not harmful for them to come out of the closet, if you will," says D'Amour. "It's the only way that they will survive. They have to expose students to the Catholic flavor they have to offer."

D'Amour says that he's most proud of how one aspect of the grant has taken on a life of its own. Every year a colloquium brings all the schools together to share common problems and solutions.

Boston College philosophy professor Peter Kreeft has described such institutions as "islands of sanity."[12] Indeed, surrounded by a sea of confusion, such islands of sanity are producing the Catholic leaders of tomorrow.

[12] Peter Kreeft, "The Liberal Arts and Sexual Morality," *Crisis*, April 2003, 21.

∞

Beyond the "Feel-Good" Message

Young Adults

*"As time passes, the Catholic Church
makes more and more sense."*

Heather Price, 31, stay-at-home
mother, Warren, Michigan

∞

By a coincidence of fate — two missed flights in December 2003 — I found myself sitting next to a young man during a flight from Memphis to Birmingham. Our discussion began with the familiar questions of origin and employment, but eventually drifted to topics of faith. A cradle Catholic, Alex admitted that although he still prayed, he hadn't been to a Catholic Church in the past six years. As we talked, it became apparent that the reason he hadn't attended was because he hadn't felt connected. Working in the banking industry, in a new city far away from family, he hadn't found a place where he felt he fit in. After speaking with folks at EWTN, I was able to put him in touch with Spirit and Truth — a young-adult group that meets for praise and worship, adoration, and fellowship every Thursday evening at St. Peter the Apostle parish in Hoover, Alabama.

This feeling of belonging or connectedness is an extremely important consideration for young Catholics.

It certainly was vital for former Evangelical Christian Heidi Saxton of Milan, Michigan. Formerly an editor with Servant Publishing, Saxton says that this longing for connectedness was the key that led her to the Catholic Church ten years ago.

Although the Catholic Church is frequently criticized by Evangelical Protestants for a perceived lack of fellowship, Saxton says that she discovered exactly the opposite.

Young and Catholic

"It was precisely this longing for community and context that led me to the Catholic Church after being involved in a variety of Evangelical Christian denominations for many years," says Saxton. "While I had encountered community in other places, this was the first time I had the sense of being a part of something larger than I could contain in my own little pea brain."

After the pastor of her Baptist church converted to Catholicism, Saxton was left with many questions. Not knowing where to turn, she obtained a copy of the *Catechism of the Catholic Church* and began reading. There she found answers to many of her questions. Her reading led her to RCIA and eventually into the Church.

It wasn't until later that she realized that she wasn't alone in her journey. Her discovery that many others around the country were coming into the Church at the same time as she did helped her realize that she was a part of something much larger — the universal Church.

"I discovered that the path which led me to the Church had been far more 'traveled by' than I ever expected," she adds.

The transformation for thirty-six-year-old Peter Nixon from Concord, California, came when he first considered the possibility of marriage in the Church.

"The first Sunday after I got to college, I slept in, and that pattern persisted for the next several years," explains Nixon of his falling away from the Church.

He describes his return to the Church as both a "push" and a "pull."

The push came when he and his then-fiancée were discussing the possibility of having a Catholic wedding.

"That forced us to answer the question of what we really believed and why," he says.

Still, Nixon says that the pull was more important.

"God got His hook into my mouth and started reeling me in. It was almost as if it had been there the whole time, the way a good fisherman gives the fish a little running room with the hook before he starts reeling in," he explains. "God had given me a few years of running room. As much as I tried to resist, there was no question I was going in the boat."

Saxon's and Nixon's stories, and those of so many others, highlight the importance of Church and community. This longing for community helps to explain the increased popularity of young-adult Catholic groups across the country.

"This pontiff has had such energy toward youth ministry," says Michelle Miller, executive director with the National Catholic Young Adult Ministry Association, which counts some two hundred organizations among its membership. "Many college students have these kinds of spiritual awakening and come into the parish, but their gifts aren't recognized. Parishes don't know what to do with twenty- and thirty-year-olds."

This lack of parish-based support for young adults has led to the growth of young-adult groups such as New York's *Love and Responsibility* discussion group, Kansas City Young Adults, Minneapolis's St. Olaf's Young Adult group, Manhattan's Contemporary Roman Catholics, Atlanta's Pure Love group, a variety of Theology of the Body discussion groups, and others around the country. The proliferation of such groups demonstrates young adults' need for both social interaction and spiritual encouragement. Scattered across the country in small cocoons of orthodoxy, these groups are providing a way for the young faithful to gather.

One characteristic many of these programs have in common is that they frequently don't take place at the local parish. Instead, they meet young adults where they are.

Young and Catholic

⚭

Going Where the Young People Are

It's a Monday night at Manhattan's Turtle Bay Grill and Lounge, and the back room of the bar is filled to capacity with young people. Although the discussion is centered on sexuality, the young adults aren't there to "hook up" with the opposite sex. They're listening to Dr. Phil Mango talk about "Love and Sex in the City: Gender Difference and Catholic Intimacy."

It's a mixture of happy hour and Catholic spirituality known as Theology on Tap, just one of many chapters nationwide that bring together young adults to learn more about the Faith. After leaving the often-insulated environments found on some college campuses, young adults in the real world long to connect with faithful peers.

"Theology on Tap shows that the young have not lost faith in the Catholic Church," says Anne Marie Wick, coordinator of the

The popular Theology on Tap allows Catholic young adults to learn about the Faith in an informal, social setting.

program in Milwaukee, where over a four-week period in 2003, more than fifteen hundred young people attended sixteen Theology on Tap events.

Started twenty-three years ago in Illinois, the organization now includes more than forty chapters in sixteen states. Theology on Tap groups gather in such cities as Atlanta, Baltimore, Chicago, Cleveland, Detroit, Lafayette, Milwaukee, Nashville, New York, Sioux Falls, Toledo, Philadelphia, and Washington, D.C.

The program is very popular in Sioux Falls, South Dakota, where between sixty and ninety people gather once a month at a country club in town.

"It's popular because it's an informal gathering where young adults can learn about their Faith," says Chris Burgwald, director of adult faith formation for the Diocese of Sioux Falls. "It doesn't have a stigma. No one would call it religious education even though that's what it is."

Burgwald says that the program answers a common need shared by young adults.

"They want to learn more about the Faith," he adds. "They want to understand why the Church teaches what it teaches and be able to explain and defend what it teaches."

Theology on Tap is but one example of the type of young-adult group that has arisen. Young-adult Catholics in New York have formed discussion groups that allow individuals to learn more about their Faith as well as demonstrate how to apply such concepts to their daily lives and relationships.

∞

Discovering Love in New York

The idea for a *Love and Responsibility* discussion group first struck foundation consultant Peter McFadden seven years ago.

Young and Catholic

McFadden had spent several years with a nonprofit organization in Europe and had returned home to New York uncertain about what to do with his life.

At the age of thirty-three, McFadden said to himself, "I'm Catholic, but what do I know about the Pope?" The only thing he could think of was, "He looks good in white."

"What a shame that I know so little about the Holy Father," thought McFadden. "Maybe if I studied his thought I would find some wisdom about what I'm supposed to do with my life."

McFadden decided to read John Paul II's classic work on human sexuality, *Love and Responsibility*, and he hasn't been the same since.

"I felt it was the greatest book ever," says McFadden, "and thought it was a shame that so few active Catholics knew about the book and its beautiful message."

Since then, McFadden has been sharing that message with others. With friend Alberto Mora, McFadden formed a young-adult discussion group centered on the book.

It took McFadden and his group of approximately forty young professionals from New York City two years to read the book together. McFadden posted summaries of the group's discussions online, and the concept has expanded from there.

The interest also led McFadden to publish a thirty-two-page magazine titled "John Paul II on *Love and Responsibility*." Members of the group distributed the magazine at World Youth Day in Toronto and during Pope Day (a celebration of John Paul II's birthday) in New York.

"Volunteers have distributed our materials in front of the White House, in front of Independence Hall, and at shopping malls in Seattle," says McFadden. "In New York alone, we had sixty enthusiastic volunteers handing out the Pope's writings on sexuality."

Today McFadden is aware of at least five other *Love and Responsibility* discussion groups, gathering in places as diverse as Boston, Saskatchewan, and Trinidad.

Another similar group is the Theology of the Body discussion group formed by Anastasia Northrop in Denver three years ago. Northrop, age twenty-six, is a member of the Russian Byzantine Eastern Catholic Church in Denver.

About a dozen members, all of whom are in their mid- to late thirties, gather with Northrop every Tuesday evening to discuss the Pope's writings on the Theology of the Body — the theological and philosophical themes of the Holy Father's first 125 Wednesday general-audience addresses. Some travel as much as an hour to attend.

Northrop says that the experience has transformed her life.

"The Theology of the Body is not only an answer to how messed up our culture is," says Northrop, "but it also presents a whole new way to understand the gospel. The more it has sunk in, the more it affects how I approach other people in general. I realize that I cannot treat people as a means to an end.

"When I read the Pope's writing," says Northrop, who handles public relations for a Denver apostolate, "I am struck by the idea that my Creator would give Himself to me."

Northrop is aware of at least twenty-five other like-minded study groups that are gathering nationwide. In fact, in January 2003 representatives from the various groups in Arizona, Dallas, Denver, Minnesota, New Orleans, and New York met in Dallas for their first Theology of the Body Forum. They met again in July in Denver to form the Theology of the Body International Alliance.

There they discussed the need for youth retreats and for pre-engagement programs on John Paul II's life-changing theology and spoke of having a presence at World Youth Day 2005 in

Young and Catholic

The Theology of the Body Forum seeks to promote the Pope's life-changing theology.

Cologne. Northrop also plans to publish a study guide titled *The Freedom and the Gift for the Theology of the Body.*

While Northrop admits that the Pope's theology can be difficult to understand, she noted the benefit of meeting as a group. "If you don't get what the Pope is saying, it's possible that someone else does."

"Young adults want to live the Faith and know what the Pope is talking about," says Northrop.

∞

Catholic in Kansas City

The need to connect with like-minded peers is what led twenty-eight-year-old Jason Osterhaus to develop Kansas City Young Adults. Raised Catholic, Osterhaus had fallen away from practicing his faith. Midway through his junior year of college at Park University in Parkville, Missouri, he began the slow process of returning to the Church.

"I had been out partying one night, and the next morning I woke up and realized that there was more to life than parties and getting drunk," he recalls.

At the time of his conversion, Osterhaus realized that he needed to leave behind his old life as well as many of his friends. He created Kansas City Young Adults in December 1999, primarily out of a need for fellowship.

"I was too old for youth groups," he explains, "but I wasn't married or in the fifty-five-and-older gang either. I perceived a gap for those people in Church ministry for those out of high school, but not yet in an older, settled role."

Through daily Mass, Osterhaus met several other young adults. Each of them, in turn, invited their peers, and the group started with approximately fifteen to twenty people meeting at various Catholic churches in the Kansas City area. Early on, the meetings involved a Bible study and eucharistic adoration, held most often at Curé of Ars or Holy Spirit parishes in Overland Park, Kansas.

Over time, the group placed monthly calendars in local churches inviting other young adults to join them. Today they have a mailing list with nearly four hundred names and draw upwards of fifty or sixty participants at the group's various weekly events. The events include eucharistic adoration on Tuesday evenings, Bible Study on Wednesdays, and a Young-Adult Mass on Thursday evening, followed by dinner and fellowship. Mass is their largest event, typically drawing as many as seventy young adults. The group gathers for social events such as movie night, camping, or retreats on weekends.

The group also engages in charitable works. Some of the young adults volunteer with the Boys and Girls Club and the Special Olympics. Others help with Meals on Wheels, and still others have organized clothing drives.

Young and Catholic

"We wanted to have as wide an opportunity for people to get involved as possible," says Osterhaus. "Someone who frequents adoration may not be the same person who desires to go work with the homeless. We're open to various faith levels."

The group has also led to the creation of a Catholic Faith and Reason apologetics group of about thirty people who meet at Our Lady of Good Counsel parish.

Young adults, says Osterhaus, are seeking to grow in their faith.

"The 'Jesus loves everyone' message is true, but young adults want something a bit more solid than that feel-good message. They have a hunger to learn more. They want to know things like why we call Mary 'mother.' "

Much of the fruit of such groups remains quiet and hidden. It's not reported on the pages of the *New York Times* or *Dallas Morning News*. Still, it goes on. Young adults are meeting one another, learning about their Faith, becoming more involved in their local parishes, embracing their baptismal gifts, entering sacramental marriages, and in many cases, discerning a call to a religious vocation as a result of their involvement in such communities. Even more promising, many of them are moving into positions of parish and diocesan leadership and effecting change at a higher level.

∞

A Minority with Attitude

Tomorrow's Catholic Leaders

"The stage is set for a revival of sorts — new leadership and a new commitment to holiness."

Jason E. Smith, 22, LAN/Systems Administrator, Washington, D.C.

Meeting for the first time at the 2001 annual Catholic Leadership Conference in Philadelphia, Catholic novelist Bud MacFarlane, Jr. and Gift Foundation president Steve Habisohn felt out of sorts.

That year's Catholic Leadership Conference had brought together leaders from more than 130 organizations. Yet as Mac-Farlane and Habisohn looked around at their fellow participants, they realized that they were among the few younger members in the group.

"Wouldn't it be great if we had something like this for young Catholic leaders?" Habisohn asked MacFarlane.

The two shook on it.

That evening, over drinks and conversation, they met with a handful of collaborators to begin planning an event that would bring together young Catholic leaders to foster friendship and working relationships. The Gift Foundation, the Mary Foundation, *Crisis* Magazine, Ave Maria Law School, and the Catholic Leadership Conference became the first supporting organizations.

Under the leadership of Carrie Gress, assistant to George Weigel and program manager for the Catholic Studies Program at the Ethics and Public Policy Center in Washington, D.C., in May 2002 more than a hundred young Catholic leaders representing over eighty Canadian and American organizations and apostolates gathered in Chicago for the first meeting of the Colebrook

Society. (A subsequent Colebrook gathering was held in November 2002 in Ontario, primarily for Canadian leaders.)

Their presence didn't register a blip on the secular media screen. In fact, it barely registered among Catholic media. Yet those in attendance could sense the Holy Spirit's presence. They understood that the gathering was about more than networking and coalition-building; it was also about building up future saints.

The three-day conference featured a variety of presentations and panel discussions examining the Catholic presence in health-care, politics, and the media. Speakers encouraged attendees to strive for personal holiness, political action, and technical competence, and to use their genius for the Church-at-large.

For many attendees, it was their first opportunity to meet with like-minded peers.

"It was very encouraging to meet these young Catholic leaders who are active in every aspect of our lives — entertainment, communications, health care, marketing, economics, and politics," says thirty-year-old Stella Marie Jeffrey, who works as director of evangelization for the Diocese of Fargo. Jeffrey attended both the 2002 and 2003 Chicago gatherings.

"If something came up, I feel that I could turn to these people, because I could trust them," adds Jeffrey.

To date, the gathering has led to more than valuable friendships: Chicago archdiocesan pro-life director Mary-Louise Kurey and attorney Brian Hengesbaugh were married in 2003 after meeting at the 2002 gathering.

In a Church beleaguered by the aftereffects of the priestly sexual-abuse scandal and frequent media attacks, the meetings have offered a much-needed occasion for young leaders to step back, witness the good that is being done in the Church, and resolve to strive for greater personal holiness.

Fr. Tad Pacholczyk, a priest in the Diocese of Fall River, Massachusetts, says he's glad to be "plugged in" to this informal network. The priest, who holds a Ph.D. from Yale, spoke at the 2002 gathering on the issues of stem-cell research and bioethics.

"I'm always inspired by young Catholic people who are on fire," says Fr. Pacholczyk. "They have a real desire to evangelize and to make use of modern means to propagate Christ. That is an inspiring thing."

Furthermore, the conference showcased the best and brightest young Catholic leaders, including Cathleen Cleaver-Ruse, U.S. Conference of Catholic Bishops Secretariat for Pro-Life Activities; Mary Hallan FioRito, vice-chancellor of the Archdiocese of Chicago; Michael Hernon, former deputy director of grassroots development for the Republican National Committee; and Barbara Nicolosi, director of Act One: Writing for Hollywood.

"I loved the philosophy behind Colebrook — fostering friendships by bringing good people together face-to-face and allowing things to bloom naturally," says Cherie Peacock, editor of *Our Sunday Visitor,* after attending the 2003 gathering.

The leaders who attend Colebrook are but a handful among the Church's best and brightest who will lead the Church into the future.

∽

From Down Under to On Top

Catholic motivational speaker Matthew Kelly was a natural choice to speak to the original Colebrook Society members in Chicago in 2002. After all, it's what he does best.

The founder of the Matthew Kelly Foundation is one of the most in-demand Catholic speakers in the world. Over the past decade, Kelly has spoken to more than two million people about

Young and Catholic

Christ and the Church. His ministry uses the timeless truths of Jesus Christ to encourage Christians to reach their full potential.

Originally from Sydney, Australia, Kelly is the fourth of eight children — all boys. Although he was born and raised Catholic, it wasn't until his late teenage years that he took an active interest in his faith at the urging of a family friend and physician.

"I always went to Church on Sunday," says Kelly, whose family frequently sat in the front pew, "but I was restless and discontent. I began to delve into the richness of Catholicism only in my late teen years."

Kelly's friend encouraged him to spend at least ten minutes in church each day. One day, while passing a church, Kelly decided to give it a try.

"It felt so peaceful that I just kept coming back," admits Kelly. "My friend later encouraged me to attend Mass at least once during the week, and it was there, in the quiet of daily Mass in my home parish in Sydney, that I learned to love the Mass.

"There," says Kelly, "I rediscovered the depth and beauty of the Mass, the timeless and timely nature of the prayers of the Mass, and the Scriptures which show that the yearning of the human heart is unchanging. Cultures change, dates and times change, but the yearning of the human heart is

Catholic motivational speaker Matthew Kelly, from Australia, has shared the Faith with more than two million people over the past decade.

always the same — a yearning for God." This, explains Kelly, is what young Catholics are truly searching for.

"They are looking for meaningful living — something beyond the pursuit of pleasure and possessions," says Kelly. "God's dream for us is that we become the best version of ourselves." He uses St. Francis of Assisi and Bl. Mother Teresa of Calcutta as examples.

"That's what they did," he says. "We are created in the image of God, born to imitate Christ, but with unique talents and unique personalities. God wants us to celebrate all of this. God wants us to become the best version of ourselves. This is holiness."

This is the message that Kelly shares, particularly with youth. He has been doing so since 1993. At the age of nineteen, while in business school, Kelly was invited to speak at a small event for approximately fifty people about what it was like to be in college, to be interested in spirituality and still be a fairly regular person. The organizer audiotaped Kelly's speech and began passing it around. Thus, Kelly's ministry was born.

Since that time, he has spoken in more than fifty countries, and he has published nine books, including *Rediscovering Catholicism* and *A Call to Joy*.

Kelly has no illusions about reaching young Catholics. He recognizes that he is competing against modern mass media.

"We have a real challenge ahead of us if we are going to engage the young people of today, and I mean engage," says Kelly. "Too much of our focus with young people in the Church over the past twenty years has been on entertainment — [albeit] a holy form of entertainment."

It's an approach that Kelly doesn't find helpful.

"This approach fails to give them the tools that will sustain them in their faith when the peer support is no longer there, or when their faith is challenged," he adds. "If young people are straying from the Church, it is because we have failed to show them that Jesus is relevant to them and their modern lives here and now in the twenty-first century. We have to show them and prove to them that following Jesus is the best way to live.

"God doesn't want us to live lives of 'quiet desperation,' but rather He wants us to live lives filled with passion and purpose," he continues. "The busy world cannot lead the young to this passion and purpose. It is discovered, nurtured, and sustained only by a life centered on the great spiritual disciplines — silence, solitude, Scriptures, and sacraments."

One apostolate in Colorado Springs, Colorado, is seeking to do just this — helping lay Catholics live a life of purpose.

∞

A Thousand Points of Light

Sherry Weddell has a bird's-eye view of the Church that most Catholics do not. A convert to Catholicism, Weddell travels the country — and the world — leading workshops with lay Catholics as codirector for the Colorado Springs–based Catherine of Siena Institute, an organization committed to helping form lay apostolates at the parish level. Since the organization's founding in 1997, the Institute has worked with more than sixteen thousand people in approximately one-quarter of the dioceses in the country. As a result, Weddell is aware of the hopeful new leadership that is just beginning in places from Atlanta to Boise.

"There truly are a 'thousand points of light' in the Catholic Church in this country," says Weddell. "I've met thousands of faithful, outstanding Catholics who are just beginning to exercise their influence for good. They are reclaiming both the fullness of the Faith and the structures of the Church."

She explains that over the past two years she has witnessed a new group of leaders beginning to emerge into their own around the country.

"The John Paul II generation is just now entering institutional leadership," she says. "The new generation of smart, creative, orthodox Catholics are starting to move into positions of real power and influence in the parochial structures: pastors, parish and diocesan staff, and religious. They are seeking each other out and forming creative alliances. These include sharp young lay women and men, newly ordained priests, and other clear, unapologetic apostles of Jesus Christ in areas such as religious education and family life.

"They are building alternate institutions and networks that are rapidly replacing the old tired, refugees-from-the-Sixties institutions. Some of the older institutions are starting to notice that dioceses are no longer coming to them. Dioceses are increasingly turning for training and advice to these up-and-coming groups for services and resources."

She offers Renew — the doctrinally weak three-and-a-half year spiritual-renewal process developed in the Archdiocese of Newark and used around the country — as one example.

"Renew is now offering an entire thirty-two-week adult formation group process that is entirely centered in the *Catechism of the Catholic Church*," she explains. "They, too, see the change and are starting to reposition themselves to the new demands."

"The tide has already turned," says Weddell. "In ten years, the difference in the Church in America as a whole will be tremendous. In twenty years, it will be dramatically different."

Not all Church watchers agree with Weddell. Some predict a steady decline for the Church. Others continue to suggest that the young are alienated from the Church. Yet, the energy and enthusiasm of those who are active suggest otherwise.

"There are those who would discount this resurgence," admits Weddell. "If you look at Catholics across the board, those who are orthodox *are* a minority, but it's a minority with attitude."

Another example of collaborative young networking to create alternative networks is the genesis of the Inaugural National Catholic Prayer Breakfast. Evangelicals have one. Hispanics have one, and women have their own too, but prior to April 28, 2004, Catholics did not have their own.

The idea originally came to Joseph Cella late in the summer of 2003.

"The call to establish a Catholic prayer breakfast struck me like a thunderclap," explains Cella. "After considering the other long-standing prayer breakfasts, I felt called to firmly plant a flag for our Faith. After all, we are the largest Church in the country and the fastest growing."

Cella approached his friend Austin Ruse, director of the New York-based Catholic Family and Human Rights Institute, and the project blossomed. Philadelphia's Cardinal Anthony Bevilacqua agreed to serve as the breakfast's Episcopal advisor.

The organization's goal is to bring Catholics from across the country together for prayer.

"There is no political agenda," says Ruse. "The focus is to thank God for His blessings upon our Church and our land. We wanted to have an event where we could invoke the Blessed Mother and the saints."

Unlike the Evangelical National Prayer Breakfast, the Catholic Breakfast is not a closed event.

"As in the Church itself, everyone is welcome, from Dr. James Dobson to Senator Ted Kennedy," explains Ruse. However, "also as in the Church, everyone is welcome, but only a few get to talk through the microphone."

The inaugural breakfast included a keynote from Cardinal Avery Dulles, as well as remarks from a handful of Democratic and Republican congressional members.

Rep. Bart Stupak (D-Mich.) told those gathered that his participation in the regular House prayer breakfast and in a Christian fellowship group give him the strength to be a Catholic first and a Democrat second.

"It's difficult to walk in the light," Stupak said. "If we walk in the light, we will love one another . . . rich and poor, born and unborn."

Sen. Rick Santorum (R-Pa.) lamented the fact that "we are the most blessed country" yet "our hearts and souls are vacuous, empty of [God's] spirit." He encouraged attendees to "get closer to God." "He is calling," said Santorum. "Let me assure you. He is calling."

"For Catholics in the New Evangelization, the breakfast is a new means of spreading the unambiguous truths of our Faith," explains Cella. "It is about prayer, fellowship, and helping the poor and most vulnerable in our society."

Attended by more than a thousand lay and religious Catholics, the inaugural breakfast was a rousing success, and attendees look forward to participating annually.

"This event is an early important part of the New Springtime for our Church in the United States," says Cella. This is only going to get bigger," he adds.

Such efforts are indicative of this country's emerging young Catholic leadership.

"We have been called the John Paul II Generation, and with good reason," wrote Peter Wolfgang, district deputy for the Knights of Columbus in an article in the *National Catholic Register*. "We are inspired by his courage and fidelity and sustained by a network of resources that have risen up under his leadership."

Young and Catholic

Wolfgang describes the new generation as one that views the Faith as a gift. "We are happy, growing in numbers and confident that the future of the Church belongs to those who are faithful to her teachings."[13]

Another example of confident young Catholic leadership is the husband-and-wife team of Soren and Ever Johnson. They're helping to bridge the gap between young Catholics and Protestants while building up the Catholic laity to evangelize the culture.

∞

Ecumenism in Action

Ever Johnson, who used to occupy Carrie Gress's role as the assistant to papal biographer George Weigel, now serves as a researcher in Weigel's Catholic Studies Project at the Ethics and Public Policy Center, a Washington, D.C., think-tank dedicated to promoting Judeo-Christian principles in public-policy debates. Soren Johnson is the communications director for the Catholic Diocese of Arlington, Virginia.

Ever grew up Catholic in Texas. She says that her Catholic Faith was the "defining essence" of her childhood in a family of twelve children. "Mom chased us out the door each day to check if we were wearing our scapulars and sprinkled us with holy water," she says. "Dad led the family Rosary every night." She admits to being a bit embarrassed as she got older by all the statues, beads, medals, and pictures, "but we loved the Church nevertheless." She says that she spent her teens and twenties seeking to understand the more perplexing doctrines of the Faith.

---

[13] Peter Wolfgang, "Attention, Peter Steinfels: You Got It Wrong." *National Catholic Register*, November 23-29, 2003, 9.

"I asked all the usual questions, but mostly with the conviction that the Church was right; even if I didn't understand how, for instance, Jesus was really present in the Eucharist." She says that wrestling with such issues helped her to embrace a more mature faith.

In graduate school, Ever studied the role of religion in international affairs. Following an internship in Vatican City, she joined Weigel as an intern and then as his research assistant, while he was working on his biography of Pope John Paul II, *Witness to Hope*.

The centerpiece of Weigel's Catholic Studies Project at EPPC is a three-week summer seminar held in Krakow, Poland, called the Tertio Millennio Seminar. The event is dedicated to teaching a new generation of cultural leaders the principles, from the Judeo-Christian tradition and especially from Catholic teaching, on which we can build a healthy culture.

Ever spent three years organizing the seminar. During that time, she became intrigued by a Chicago applicant, Soren Johnson. He was from a strong, nondenominational, Evangelical Protestant background, but he had had a powerful experience of traditional Christianity in the Orthodox churches while living and working in Russia. With a theology degree from an Orthodox seminary, and on his way to being a master of divinity at Princeton Seminary, Soren had intended to become an "ecumenically sensitive" Protestant pastor. That was before he looked into Catholicism, where he eventually found his true home.

"I put his application at the top of the list and looked forward to meeting him," recalls Ever. After meeting, they developed a mutual interest in each other, and "three weeks in the romantic city of Krakow decided our fate." They were married the next year.

Young and Catholic

Ever thinks of their meeting and marriage as the culmination of a way of understanding the Faith that she had been seeking for years. Through her work on the board of the now-defunct Regeneration Forum, an ecumenical group of young Christians who sought to integrate faith and culture, she had experienced how disunity in the Church makes the gospel message difficult to preach in the world.

"Because of schism and dissension in the Church, the gospel message is garbled and confusing to those who don't already have an experience of Christ," she says. "How can Christians expect to be light and salt in the world when they don't agree with each other enough to commune at the same table?"

Soren and Ever Johnson are excited about the possibilities for ecumenical dialogue and the enculturation of the gospel in various cultures.

"What we see among younger Christians of varying traditions are grassroots movements, working together on social issues that they already agree on, especially pro-life issues," adds Ever.

The Johnsons believe that as such groups come to know and trust one another, a new environment of willingness and open-mindedness will be created.

"As Christians of varying traditions experience each other as fellow brothers and sisters in Christ, and so begin to personally feel the pain of the divisions, doctrinal discussions may come to seem more worthwhile to a sizable-enough segment of the Church to jumpstart official dialogues. We'd like to be there to help translate the Faith in a way that people coming at it from very different places can agree to and understand."

To that end, both Johnsons hope their work will bring together Protestants, Catholics, and Orthodox to change the future of the Church.

Tomorrow's Catholic Leaders

"We want to challenge young Christians to a more radical commitment to a truly Christian lifestyle, to respect and learn from Christians of other traditions, and thus to develop a healthier way to preach the gospel for the sake of our culture and the world."

∝

Catholic Is Who I Am

World Youth Day

*"Pope John Paul II is such a great man
and role model. Even though he is old, he
inspires the young. He builds our faith."*

Nicola-Martiza Coombs, 18,
student, Trinidad and Tobago

∞

At the 2002 World Youth Day, held July 18-28, more than a thousand young people from several countries packed into the Toronto exhibit hall sporting brightly colored T-shirts of aqua, lemon, orange, red, and blue.

While most of the teens and young adults were enjoying the NET-team presentation taking place on the center stage, others continued to stream toward the perimeter. Ringing the outer walls of the auditorium stood hundreds of youth. There, twenty-five makeshift purple confessional booths had been set up along the walls. Young people lined up five to ten deep, reading the examination of conscience in their pilgrimage prayer guides as they waited for the sacrament of Reconciliation. Confession was in high demand.

"While waiting for Confession myself, I was pulled out of line three times by youth asking me to hear their confessions," said Fr. Greg Paffel, thirty-five, pastor of St. John's Catholic Church in Foley, Minnesota.

The scene was repeated at most of World Youth Day's venues, where some one thousand priests heard confessions over a ten-day period. They offered the sacrament within their pilgrimage groups, in Toronto's exhibit halls, at Coronation Park — which had been temporarily renamed *Duc in Altum* ("put out into the deep") Park — and at Downsview Lands Park, where the final papal Mass was celebrated.

Young and Catholic

World Youth Day, perhaps more than anything else, exemplifies what it means to be young and Catholic. For it is there that one comes face-to-face with the future of the worldwide Church.

Karol Wojtyla has always enjoyed spending time with the young. As a priest and bishop, he frequently went camping and hiking with the youth. Even today, despite his age, he sees himself as young at heart.

Digressing from his prepared remarks, Pope John Paul II asked the crowd during his 2003 visit to Spain, "How old is the Pope?"

"Almost eighty-three," he continued after a pause, then added, "A young person of eighty-three."

At World Youth Day in Toronto, he told the youth, "The aged Pope is full of years, but young at heart."

Modern youth have enthusiastically responded to his call. For nineteen years, more than eleven million youth have accepted the invitation to spend a week with the Holy Father. They show up in droves bearing signs and chanting slogans of "John Paul II, we love you." Their commitment speaks volumes about the younger generation and the direction in which they are headed.

∞

Meeting the Universal Church

The young cannot help but be impressed by the global sea of humanity present at World Youth Day. Americans sit next to Brazilians, Australians next to Poles, and Kenyans next to Indians. The pilgrims frequently carry journals, recording the names and addresses of those they meet along the way.

"It's wonderful to see youth from all over the world again," said Ana-Maria Cagalj, twenty-six, of Bosnia-Herzegovina, who came dressed in a traditional Northern Bosnia dress adorned with gold coins. She has attended three World Youth Days.

"When we welcomed the Pope, I was struck by the procession of flags," said Fr. Paffel. "A representative from each country knelt before the Holy Father, and he blessed them, and I thought 'every nation will bow' to Jesus Christ. That was an awesome thing to see."

Sixteen-year-old John Marotta of Atlanta spoke of meeting people from Italy, Ireland, South Africa, Germany, and France. "We all share the same love for the Church and the Holy Father," said Marotta.

The value of such global solidarity was not lost on observers.

"This provides an opportunity for a significant portion of the Church to see that the Church is a global community," said Carl Anderson, president of the Knights of Columbus. "Rich countries meeting their counterparts in poorer countries. This will change the reality of the Church for the future."

∞

Connecting with the Sacraments

The youth use World Youth Day as an opportunity to connect with Christ through the sacraments, particularly Reconciliation and the Eucharist. Not only did local priests offer daily Mass with their pilgrimage groups, but World Youth Day builds up to the final papal Mass celebrated on Sunday, the last day of the encounter. In addition to daily celebrations of the Eucharist, many of the event's venues had eucharistic adoration hosted by youth groups such as Youth 2000 and NET Ministries.

Molly O'Neill of Houston, Texas, twenty-three, spoke about the power of eucharistic adoration that was held one evening in an exhibit hall.

"To walk into the hall and see tens of thousands of sixteen- and seventeen-year-olds in adoration was a real highlight for me," said O'Neill. "My faith became real to me."

Young and Catholic

Nicola-Martiza Coombs of Trinidad and Tobago, eighteen, used her time in adoration to think of her family back home. "I prayed for my family and for the success of World Youth Day. I prayed to be in union with Jesus Christ," said Coombs.

Large-scale individual Confession was first given a prominent role at the Circus Maximus at World Youth Day 2000 in Rome. So convinced of the sacrament's value, the Knights of Columbus contributed a million dollars to World Youth Day in Toronto specifically for the purchase of 1,500 Chiapas stoles, the construction of the purple confessionals, and training for the sacrament.

Knights of Columbus president Carl Anderson said he was extremely encouraged by the large numbers of youth attending Confession. "The Holy Father asks us to remain youthful and regain our youthfulness. One way to regain our youthfulness is through Reconciliation," said Anderson. "An encounter with the Lord is always a new beginning and that is what the sacrament of Reconciliation is all about. The sacrament is at the heart of World Youth Day, and the Reconciliation areas are at the heart of this encounter."

"In this day and age, the fact that an infirm old man can bring together so many people in the name of the gospel, in the name of goodness and peace, is a miracle," said Fr. Thomas Rosica, CEO and national director of World Youth Day 2002.

Following Denver's World Youth Day in August 1993, then-Archbishop James Francis Stafford had been invited to Rome for a meeting of the Plenarium of the Congregation for the Doctrine of the Faith. After the meeting, Pope John Paul II greeted Archbishop Stafford in Italian.

"Ah! Denver, Denver, *una rivoluzione! Una rivoluzione!*" the Holy Father said with a wide smile.

Cardinal Stafford admits that he wasn't clear at first about the Pope's use of the word *revolution*. "What had he meant when he said that the experience of the Denver World Youth Day was 'a revolution' for him?" he wondered.

The matter was cleared up later when Cardinal Stafford shared it with a member of the Papal Household, a priest who is a friend of the Holy Father.

"Before Denver, the Pope and members of the Roman Curia had looked toward the East for the renewal of the Church; he believed, '*Lux ex Oriente* — light would be coming from the East,' " explained the priest. "But after his experience of young people in Denver, he now saw that 'light would be dawning also from the West — *Lux ex Occidente.*' That was the revolution! The light of Jesus had shown on the faces of those young Americans. I pray every day that the Pope's revolution will come about."

One could argue that the revolution has already begun.

∞

Eleven Years after Denver

Sherry Weddell believes World Youth Day was "the turning point for the Church in Denver."

Eleven years ago, hundreds of thousands of youth converged on the city of Denver to celebrate the first World Youth Day held in the United States. The seeds that were planted there continue to sprout. They are blooming in the increased number of young adults embracing the sacraments, the growth of lay movements in Denver and beyond, and the vocations that resulted from the event.

"When the Pope came to Denver, many people were saying that the young of America would not care for the Pope . . . that the young here were very secular," says Msgr. Edward Buelt, pastor of Our Lady of Loretto in Foxfield, Colorado. "Denver proved that that was baloney. The Pope received an extraordinary welcome," he adds.

Young and Catholic

More than two hundred thousand young people responded to the Holy Father's invitation to World Youth Day in Denver.

"World Youth Day in Denver brought about an extraordinary amount of conversions," says Msgr. Buelt, who chaired the 1993 World Youth Day Planning Committee. He recalls running into an elderly American couple in 1998. "The grandmother began to cry as she explained that her granddaughter had attended World Youth Day in Denver five years before.

" 'Our family has never been the same since she came home,' she tearfully recounted," says Msgr. Buelt. "World Youth Day instilled the Holy Spirit in many, many families."

That Spirit can especially be seen in the increased popularity of youth and young-adult ministry programs, as were previously discussed.

"There has been tremendous growth in youth ministry, to the point where in Denver it's really cool to be a young adult or youthful Catholic," says Roxanne King, editor of the *Denver Catholic Register*. "If you're a teen and are Catholic, it's easy to find a place where you can belong and be supported. There are very dynamic youth programs at many of the parishes."

Among them is the presence of the Life Teen program at St. Frances Cabrini Catholic Church in Littleton.

"Before Life Teen, there was only a small group of youth," explains Jim Beckman, director of youth ministry at St. Frances Cabrini. "Now every Sunday we have more than four hundred youth at our Sunday evening Mass."

"While there were some good things happening prior to 1993, World Youth Day really opened the floodgates," says Beckman. As examples, he offered the National Catholic Youth Conference (NCYC) and the Franciscan University of Steubenville youth summer conferences.

"Prior to World Youth Day, NCYC would be attended by two to three thousand youth," explains Beckman. More than twenty-three thousand youth attended the organization's fall 2003 conference in Houston.

Franciscan University of Steubenville has also witnessed an upsurge in attendance at their summer youth conferences. When the university held its first youth conference in 1976, one thousand teens attended, and the numbers grew every year thereafter.

"By 1994 we had three conferences. We expected two thousand youth for each, and ended up with over three thousand," says Lisa Ferguson, director of public relations for the university.

The conferences outgrew the campus, and eventually the university began to offer regional conferences. During the summer of 2003, they hosted more than thirty thousand youth at thirteen

A Catholic youth joins fellow Life Teen members in prayer.

conferences in Arizona, California, Colorado, Georgia, Louisiana, Ohio, Massachusetts, Minnesota, Missouri, and South Carolina.

Youth 2000 USA has noticed the trend as well. Since 1992, the Dallas-based apostolate has offered more than 350 youth weekend retreats focused on the Eucharist across the United States, in Africa, Argentina, Australia, Canada, Panama, Poland, and Sweden.

"We first received permission from the World Youth Day committee to have eucharistic adoration in Denver," says U.S. national director Anne Brawley. "Since then we have been responsible for adoration at all subsequent World Youth Days. In Toronto adoration was held in the main Exhibition Center, and there were more than a thousand young people in attendance at all times."

Cardinal Stafford, speaking to the *Denver Catholic Register,* said that Archbishop Charles Chaput has also noticed a renewal of the sacrament of Reconciliation over the past few years. Archbishop Chaput has been impressed by the hundreds of committed young people who join him for Mass every Sunday evening.

Another fruit that former Denver archbishop Cardinal Stafford attributed to World Youth Day is the rise of ecclesial lay movements. In Denver alone, the Neocatechumenal Way, the Community of the Beatitudes, the Marian Community of Reconciliation (Fraternidad), and Sodalitium Christianae Vitae (Christian Life Movement) have taken hold.

"Those communities clearly are the fruit of World Youth Day," says Cardinal Stafford, who now serves as president of the Pontifical Council for the Laity.

∞

Salt in the City

"After returning from World Youth Day in Denver, several of us formed a prayer group," says John-Henry Westen, editor of

LifeSite News, an online pro-life news service. "Almost all of those people are now leading different Catholic apostolates or doing something significant for the Church."

World Youth Day in Toronto was key for Peter McFadden's *Love and Responsibility* group as well.

"The Pope asked us to be salt for the earth," recalls McFadden. "While we were driving home from Toronto, we spent the first half of the trip regretting leaving Toronto. The second half, we tried to imagine being salt for the earth in New York, and resolved to be Salt in the City."

Since that time, McFadden has started the Pope Day celebration, First Saturday Rosary pilgrimages through the Churches of New York City, and an ambitious Pre-Cana and Natural Family Planning program through Our Savior's Catholic Church.

Such efforts have led not only to evangelization efforts, but also to marriage. Several of the group's original members, including its co-founders, have recently become engaged.

"That's happening to a lot of us," says McFadden with a smile. "We take that as a sign that God is trying to raise an army."

At the age of sixteen, Steven Maas attended World Youth Day in Denver with thirty people from his parish, St. Joseph's Catholic Church in West St. Paul, Minnesota.

The highlight for him was realizing that the Church was much bigger than he realized.

"There were hundreds of thousands of other Catholics my age who believed the same things that I did," says Maas. "It was then that I realized that the Church was a whole lot bigger than just the handful of young people at my own parish."

World Youth Day spurred Maas on to greater involvement in his youth group at church and a greater desire to make his faith his own. His desire to learn more about the Faith of his youth led him to the Catholic Studies program at the University of St. Thomas. After graduating from that program, Maas later joined with Br. Peter Gabriel to produce a "reality"-style video of World Youth Day in Rome. They've used the resulting video, "Don't Turn Back," to encourage youth to attend World Youth Day in Toronto.

Perhaps the most obvious fruits of World Youth Day, however, have been religious vocations — not only to Denver's seminaries, Redemptoris Mater Missionary Seminary, and St. John Vianney Theological Seminary, but elsewhere as well.

This was made abundantly clear to me during a telephone interview I conducted with Sr. John Paul of the Ann Arbor–based Sisters of Mary, Mother of the Eucharist, while writing a story for the *National Catholic Register*.

During the course of our conversation, Sr. John Paul described how World Youth Day, and the Holy Father's words to the young gathered in Denver, had been the turning point in discerning her own religious vocation as a nun. After she had patiently answered all of my questions, she told me, "Hold on. There's another sister here whom you need to talk to." That sister told a strikingly similar story of discerning her vocation as a result of the Denver gathering.

However, the phone call didn't end there. That sister proceeded to pass the phone to another, and she passed it on to still another. Nearly an hour later, by the time I was finished interviewing all of them, I had spoken to four young religious sisters from a relatively recent religious community, all from different states and each of whom felt particularly moved by her experience in Denver.

While a sophomore at Franciscan University of Steubenville, Sr. John Paul led a group on one of sixteen pilgrimage buses from Ohio to World Youth Day in Denver.

Sr. John Paul contrasted her experience in Denver with her first encounter with Pope John Paul II. She had first been in the presence of the Pope six years earlier, when the Holy Father met Billy Graham at South Carolina's Williams Brice Stadium on September 11, 1987.

"I was in junior high," says Sr. John Paul. "Most of the people were there to see Billy Graham, so when the Holy Father appeared, there wasn't much of a response. No one was yelling, 'We love the Pope.' "

Thus, Sr. John Paul didn't know what to expect in Denver.

"Looking back at World Youth Day in Denver, what impacted me the most was how the Holy Father related to the young people," says Sr. John Paul. "We were all screaming, 'John Paul II, we love you,' and he grinned at us and replied, 'John Paul II, he loves you.' My vocation is a direct response to John Paul II's presence in the Church and his call to the young people."

Also on one of the Steubenville buses was Joseph Dean of Laurel, Maryland, then twenty-three years old. While on the trip, Dean first met the Franciscan Friars of Renewal, who were providing spiritual direction for the pilgrims.

"I was impressed by their joy, their fraternity, and their prayerfulness," recalls Fr. Joseph Mary Dean. "Growing up among your friends, you might not see anyone who is your age and is in love with the Church, so being with the friars and hundreds of thousands of young people who were on fire with their faith gives you the inspiration and courage to do it yourself."

Dean's experiences on the trip and in Denver led him to discern a religious vocation. In March of the following year, he visited the friars and later joined them. He is one of at least two friars (among one hundred in the order) tracing their vocation to World Youth Day in Denver. Fr. Joseph Mary was ordained on May 19, 2003.

Young and Catholic

Among other things, one of the innovative aspects of Denver's World Youth Day was the introduction of days of catechesis provided for youth by bishops from around the world, an aspect of World Youth Day that has been recreated at all subsequent World Youth Day gatherings.

"The catechetical sessions in Mile High Stadium made a big impact on me," says Sr. Mary Catherine, who professed her first vows with the Sisters of Mary, Mother of the Eucharist, on August 6, 2003. "The entire event planted seeds."

Similar stories are just now beginning to be told as a result of the 2002 World Youth Day in Toronto.

"There is a resurgence of youthfulness and enthusiasm among the youth in their involvement in their communities," says Robert Légère, now twenty years old, who portrayed Jesus during the Way of the Cross along Toronto's University Avenue during World Youth Day. "The light of faith is burning brighter in our churches."[14]

Already, World Youth Day in Toronto has led to the creation of Canada's first Catholic broadcast television network, Salt and Light. Housed in the former World Youth Day offices, and headed by Fr. Thomas Rosica, the former CEO and national director of World Youth Day 2002, the network is bringing the Faith to a country where the Church has been weakened.

"The time was ripe for this," says Fr. Rosica. "We really have moved very far away from our roots in the name of being politically correct and tolerant. In order to conform to the culture and society, we have forgotten who we are. World Youth Day was a wake-up call, and the young people are the ones who will lead us

---

[14] "Interview with Robert Légère, Who Depicted Jesus in the Stations," *Zenit*, December 25, 2002.

back. Pope John Paul made that very clear, and the youth were energized by it."

Of the twenty-two people on Salt and Light's staff, the majority are young people who were helping to plan and organize World Youth Day.

"Goodness and light, beauty and truth attract," says Fr. Rosica. "I've never felt the zest and joy of evangelization as I have from [the young]."

While the youth attended the event in the bright colors of teen fashion, World Youth Day's religious came dressed in colors of their own — black or blue clerics and habits in various shades of brown, blue, gray, black, and white.

Br. Pio Maria of the Franciscan Friars of the Renewal said that the interest in religious vocations in Toronto was great.

"I couldn't go twenty feet without someone taking my picture, asking me my name, or asking me about my vocation — even in the bathroom," says Br. Pio.

One young woman considered her attendance at World Youth Day as part of her discernment process.

"Prior to World Youth Day, I began feeling a call toward the religious life," says Paula Rooney, twenty-one, of Elrosa, Minnesota. While there, Rooney was able to speak with the Carmelites at the vocation pavilion. Since that time, she has attended a come-and-visit weekend with the Poor Clares and is discerning a possible religious vocation.

"I've particularly noticed an increased interest in vocations among men, looking at the priesthood," said Jennifer Brennan, campus minister at the University of Toledo. "They seem to be seeking an identity that allows them to be uniquely Catholic."

Bishop George Lucas, of Springfield, Illinois, has had many youth ask him about his own vocation, particularly following his

Friday-morning catechesis session. He recalls a story that a fellow bishop had related to him.

"He told me of a young man entering the seminary this year," says Bishop Lucas. "The seminarian had been at World Youth Day in Rome and said it had made a difference for him. There has been a real openness among youth to do whatever God is calling them to do."

At Toronto's Sunday-morning Mass, Pope John Paul encouraged the youth to consider religious life.

"If you love Jesus, love the Church," the Holy Father said. "Do not be discouraged by the sins and failings of some of her members, but think of the vast majority of dedicated and generous priests and religious whose only wish is to serve and do good. There are many priests, sisters, and consecrated persons here today. Be close to them and support them. If in the depths of your hearts you feel the same call, do not be afraid to follow Christ on the royal road of the Cross."

Although it's still too early to tell, some seem to be responding.

"We have at least one new seminarian who traces his vocation to Toronto," says Fr. Matthew Gamber, former associate director of university ministry at Gonzaga University in Spokane and currently a priest in the Archdiocese of Chicago.

Pope John Paul II's distinct relationship with the young has been apparent from the very start. He said as much during his Angelus message on the twenty-fifth anniversary of his pontificate, on October 13, 2003: "Now, while I think with gratitude of the past, my thoughts turn to young people, with whom I established, right from the start of my Petrine ministry, a preferential dialogue. I remember that, at the end of that first Angelus, I added a special greeting for them, saying, 'You are the future of the world; you are the hope of the Church; you are my hope.' "

"I must recognize," John Paul II said in conclusion, "that the response by young people has been truly encouraging. Today I wish to thank them for always having been close to me during these years, and I would like them to know that I continue to count on them."

There is the commonly held belief that the young are cynical and jaded by their constant exposure to morally corrupt music, television, and motion pictures. Some argue that because of this, the young cannot identify with the Church or its leaders. In the book *Virtual Faith: The Irreverent Spiritual Quest of Generation X*, Tom Beaudoin laments Generation X's apathy toward authority by saying that his generation would "never weep in public for the memory of a great leader."[15]

Yet at World Youth Day, I saw the young frequently weep publicly in the presence of Pope John Paul II.

The crying was first evident upon John Paul's arrival in Toronto, as he slowly and unexpectedly walked down the airplane's stairs with little assistance. The prime minister's wife had tears streaming down her face, and there were no dry eyes even in the media pool. A young girl, one of the first to meet the Pope, burst into tears.

There were tears as the Holy Father blessed a group of mentally handicapped people from his boat on Lake Simcoe — even in the eyes of those watching with binoculars from a distant shore.

On July 27, the Pope was scheduled to meet with Canada's politicos. Along his way, he saw a group gathered at the fence at Morrow Park. He stopped the golf cart to greet them, and a two-year-old girl was brought to him. He kissed and blessed her. And again, there were tears.

---

[15] Tom Beaudoin, *Virtual Faith: The Irreverent Spiritual Quest of Generation X* (San Francisco: Jossey-Bass, 1998), 10.

"Being in the presence of the Holy Father and hearing him speak — it is like he is speaking to each one of us individually about his love for us," says Atlanta's Katie Orlando. "It brought me to tears how much he believes in us and loves us and the Church. It gave me hope and inspiration. I'm proud to be Catholic and to stand up in the midst of controversy and say that I love being Catholic. It's who I am."

Not only is John Paul II the only pope the young have ever known, but they recognize the truths of Christ and His Church in him. They need him. They share his sorrow. They feel with him. They are grateful to him, and each time they are with him, they think they are seeing him for the last time. They wonder how they will ever get along without him, and so they cry tears of joy and sorrow.

Contrary to Beaudoin's observation, when God calls the Holy Father home, Generations X and Y will most assuredly weep in public for the memory of a great leader.

∞

Bathed in a Culture of Life
The International Catholic Youth Movement

*"I love the fact that the Church is universal.
It's found all over the earth, and there's
a place for everyone and everyone's gifts."*

Nicole Stallworth, 28, stay-at-home
mother, Byron, Georgia

∞

As demonstrated by World Youth Day, the youthful enthusiasm for the Catholic Faith is not exclusive to the United States. Catholic young adults around the world are embracing the true meaning of the word *catholic*. Youth involved in various international Catholic movements have gathered for the past decade in such locales as Rome, Mexico, Europe, Poland, and the Philippines. In fact, one of the largest gatherings of youth ever assembled took place at 1995's World Youth Day in Manila. There, more than four million youth gathered to hear the Holy Father's message.

The Church knows no boundaries. Young Catholics around the world are being attracted to the Church for the same reasons as youth in the United States are.

∞

The Church Down Under

When David Schutz overheard some elderly nuns complaining about the lack of vocations in Australia, he couldn't resist offering his perspective. Schutz, a former Lutheran pastor and convert to the Catholic Faith, works with Catholic Adult Education for the diocese of Melbourne and the Melbourne Catholic Ecumenical and Inter-faith Commission.

"I told them that as far as I could see, there was a healthy influx of new vocations," says Schutz. "They said, 'Yes, but not the right sort.'" By this the sisters meant that these new priests and nuns wholeheartedly supported the Pope and the magisterial teachings of the Church. Such acceptance of Church teaching is common among young religious and laypeople both in the United States and abroad.

"We are seeing a strong resurgence of young men entering the priesthood here locally," says Schutz. "The Dominicans are especially drawing newcomers."

The attraction to the Dominicans may be due, in part, to the elevation of Dominican Fr. Anthony Fisher as Sydney auxiliary bishop. Described, even by himself, as the "baby bishop," Fisher is Australia's youngest bishop, at the age of forty-four.

"All the new vocations are conservative Catholics, intentionally faithful to the Magisterium," adds Schutz.

"In the archdiocesan center where I work, a number of offices are dominated by young, vibrant, and committed Catholics, especially the youth office and the vocations office," he continues. "Our own Catholic Adult Education Melbourne also has a number of younger Catholics in their twenties working — and eager to work — for us. World Youth Day has had a great effect."

It is a trend that has been noted by others in Australia as well.

"The situation in Melbourne is very exciting," says James Mc-Donald, director of Catholic Youth Ministry for the Melbourne Archdiocese. "A new generation of Catholic youth have been inspired to earnestly seek Christ through the depth of Catholic tradition. They love Christ; they love the Pope; they love the Church; they love the sacraments while maintaining a personalistic experience of God in their practice of the Faith."

In a report prepared for Archbishop Denis Hart's 2004 *ad limina* visit to Rome, McDonald notes forty-six active youth groups, twenty-eight young-adult groups, and forty-three other ministry and outreach groups serving youth. Retreat ministries such as NET, Catholic Youth Ministry, Disciple's Youth Mission Team, and others are also very active in the archdiocese.

"Youth group leaders, parish and diocesan youth workers, and other leadership positions are being filled by these youth," says McDonald. "This is a sign of hope and vitality for the Church in Melbourne."

Not all are so hopeful about the Church's future in Australia.

Professor Richard Rymarz suggests a more cautious tone. He believes that the short-term future of the Church in Australia holds increasing decline.

"My own research on core Catholic adolescents suggests quite strongly that youth who are involved in parishes are moving away from Catholic belief and practice," says Rymarz, who is the Cardinal George Pell Lecturer in Religious Education at the Australian Catholic University.

The 2001 National Church Life Survey bears Rymarz's observations out. According to the survey, only fifteen percent of baptized Australian Catholics, of any age, practice their faith, and the practice rate of young adults after leaving Catholic schools is less than five percent.

Still, others are bolstered by the promising efforts among Australia's active young Catholics. Clara Geoghegan admits that the Church in Australia is not attracting large numbers of young people, but she says that those who continue to practice, or return to practice, faithfully accept the teaching of the Church.

"They are searching for that which is authentic in the Catholic tradition," says Geoghegan, who works as education and project officer with Catholic Adult Education Melbourne. "They judge priests and bishops on their sincerity. Most who have met Cardinal Pell love him."

Young and Catholic

She adds that while some describe Cardinal Pell as conservative because of his support for the Holy Father and the Church's teachings, such labels are meaningless to the young.

"The young often return to the Church in search of a moral code and an authentic spirituality," she says. "Issues such as sexual promiscuity, abortion, drugs, and youth suicide cannot be avoided by young people today. Many young people have been touched by these issues either through their own experiences or those of friends and family and are seeking viable alternatives and an authentic way of life."

The impact of vibrant young Catholics in Australia can most readily be seen in efforts such as the John Paul II Institute, devotional practices, Carnivale Christi, and the 2001 founding of Campion College of Australia.

"While the numbers of youth embracing Catholicism are still numerically small considered against the statistics of the numbers of people who are nominally Catholic, those who are interested are certainly interested in orthodox Catholicism and have primarily been inspired by the Pope," says Dr. Tracey Rowland, dean of the John Paul II Institute for Marriage and Family in Australia.

"They are very generous and many are considering vocations to religious life," adds Rowland. "This is a definite improvement from my own immediate post-conciliar generation who were the guinea pigs in the post-conciliar experiments, and who mostly fell by the wayside altogether."

Opened in July 2001, the John Paul II Institute has enrolled over 250 students. Of those, Rowland says, the majority have been in their mid- to late twenties. It is one of ten campuses around the world affiliated with the Pontifical Lateran University in Rome. The campus was erected in Melbourne at the urging of Pope John Paul for the defense of family life and the sanctity of human life.

The International Catholic Youth Movement

"The John Paul II Institute," Dr. Rowland says, "will help educate a whole new generation of Catholics, mostly laity."

"These young Catholics are branded as conservative by the baby-boomer generation," explains Geoghegan, "but this is a misreading of the situation by people who are imposing their own experiences and prejudices rather than attempting to understand the emergence of a new Catholic paradigm."

As two examples, Melbourne has two active Theology of the Body discussion groups, and an hour of eucharistic adoration at Melbourne's St. Patrick's Cathedral draws two hundred young people every Thursday evening.

Rowland attributes the paradigm shift to the generational differences. "Whereas the 1960s generation had something to rebel against, the so-called X generation is rebelling against the liberalism and consequent nihilism of the 1960s generation," she says.

Geoghegan agrees.

"My own generation took a very intellectual approach to our Faith," says Geoghegan. "We were responding to the liberal and dissident Catholics who were prevalent in Church and educational bureaucracies in the 1970s and were implementing a secularist interpretation of faith."

The younger generations, she says, "have demonstrated a more 'affective' approach to the Church."

"They are drawn by the prayer traditions," Geoghegan adds.

In 2001 and again in 2002, young Catholics in Sydney combined their artistic talents at Carnivale Christi, a three-week event featuring the richness of Christian drama, music, poetry, and art. The event attracted more than two hundred performers and an audience of over four thousand.

Entirely a youth initiative, the Carnivale was organized by the Sydney Archdiocese Youth Events Committee, the Society of St.

Young and Catholic

Peter, Life/Theatre, and Sydney University Catholic Chaplaincy under the direction of twenty-two-year-old Anthony McCarthy.

Initiatives such as eucharistic adoration, Scripture studies, Theology of the Body courses and discussion groups, and Life Week have been well attended by young adults on the campus of the University of Sydney.

The future of the Church in Australia, Dr. Rowland concludes, "depends much upon the situation in the seminaries and upon whether the new generation of bishops are chosen from among the conciliar generation of priests, or whether this generation is 'skipped' and the younger men who have been inspired more by the teachings of the Pope, than by the spirit of the Sixties, are given a chance to lead."

"Numerically, the Church in Australia is dwindling and will shrink rapidly in the next twenty years," Geoghegan says. "But the young are well networked and could provide significant future leadership. I see the future of the Church in Australia as being small but dynamic."

∞

More Signs from around the Globe

Similar results can be observed elsewhere.

In Paris in December 2002, approximately eighty thousand young people gathered as part of the Taizé Community's twenty-fifth European Meeting. Since 1978, the annual event has attracted as many as one hundred thousand young people at gatherings in France, India, the Philippines, and South Africa.

"This gathering is a sign of hope for our world," John Paul II told those gathered in Paris. "It shows that the young of today are thirsting for truth, happiness, beauty, and for an absolute, and that they are striving to give meaning to their lives."

The International Catholic Youth Movement

"In regular prayer, by reading the Scriptures diligently, by a strong sacramental life, the young will encounter Christ, who will show them the Father's face of kindly love and who will manifest His presence to them throughout their lives," the Pope added.

Half a world away, in June 2003, more than ten thousand youth from Mexico gathered to take part in the eighth National Missionary Youth Congress (CONAJUM). Their message: "Youth of the New Millennium, Do Not Be Afraid to Carry the Gospel to the World!" Organized by the Church in Mexico, CONAJUM was first held in 1982 and has been held every three years.

The young are also responding to the Holy Father's call in Poland. According to papal biographer George Weigel, Krakow's Dominican Basilica of the Holy Trinity is packed with three thousand young people for its Sunday-evening Masses.[16]

Fr. Waclaw Jamroz, originally from Poland, says that the Church has had no difficulty in generating religious vocations in the Pope's native country. "There are so many that they are able to send some to the United States," says Fr. Jamroz, who serves as the Catholic chaplain at Chicago's Midway Airport. Weigel corroborates Fr. Jamroz's findings, claiming that one-third of all European seminarians today are in Poland.[17]

The greatest growth in the Church has taken place elsewhere. By 2025, Penn State historian Philip Jenkins estimates that almost three-quarters of world Catholics will be found in Africa, Asia, and Latin America. In Africa alone, notes Weigel, there were sixteen million Catholics in the early 1950s. Today, there are 120 million. By 2050, there may be as many as 240 million.

[16] George Weigel, *Letters to a Young Catholic* (New York: Basic Books, 2004), 227.
[17] Ibid., 236.

Young and Catholic

Whether in Poland, France, Mexico, Australia, Africa, or India, young adults are drawn to the universal truths expressed through Christ and His Church.

"I love the solid theological, logical, and philosophical foundations upon which the Church is built," explains Joseph Kensy, a twenty-two-year-old analyst from Delhi, India, who maintains the web log *Catholics in India*. Kensy's website began as a secular web log devoted to dealing with Indian politics, but has slowly gravitated toward more Catholic topics.

Kensy says that the Second Vatican Council document *Nostra Aetate*, in particular, rekindled his faith.

"The Second Vatican Council clarified the Catholic's role in the modern world, in laymen's terms," says Kensy. In addition to being a member of his parish youth group, Kensy also serves as secretary for his parish council.

"I'm the youngest member," adds Kensy. "The nearest member [in age] is nearly twice my age."

Kensy says that the priestly sexual-abuse scandals of 2002 had not impacted his faith. He views the scandals as a uniquely American problem.

"We view the scandals as a problem of the Catholic Church in America," says Kensy. "We view them as being the outcome of sociocultural norms prevalent in American society today."

∽

Shaping Language
at the United Nations

Perhaps even more surprising than the pockets of youth worldwide who are embracing the Church is the fact that many with a Catholic worldview are influencing current public policy on a global scale.

The International Catholic Youth Movement

Through the work of the New York–based World Youth Alliance, young people from around the globe are having a significant impact on the language being used at the United Nations. While not specifically Catholic, the World Youth Alliance is an example of how youth with a Catholic worldview are changing international public policy.

The World Youth Alliance began in 1999 when a handful of youth, under the leadership of then-twenty-one-year-old Toronto-born Anna Halpine, presented their ideas at the U.N. conference on population and development. Halpine had followed the 1994 and 1995 conferences in Cairo and Beijing and was familiar with the language being used and the ideas being presented by the Clinton administration's delegation.

"They were bringing in young people to advance an extreme agenda of sexual rights and a narrow idea of the human person and human family, and saying that they spoke for the world's three billion young people," recalls Halpine, who had been finishing up her undergraduate music studies in New York. "The youth were being used as pawns."

The following morning, March 26, 1999, Halpine led a group of young people, including Diana Kilarjian and Charlie Hoare of London. The group presented alternative ideas they felt most young people would embrace, and the World Youth Alliance was born.

"They determined that there needed to be a unified front for young people to let the delegates know that the young people who were speaking for everyone were not speaking for everyone," explains Austin Ruse, president of the Catholic Family and Human Rights Institute.

Ever since, the organization has grown. What started with just a handful of youth has now grown to more than a million members from a hundred countries.

The Alliance is organized regionally to allow its members to respond to concerns on a local, grassroots level. In addition to their New York headquarters, the organization operates offices in Mexico City serving Latin America, in Brussels serving Europe, and in Nairobi serving Africa. They also have a standing committee that serves Asia. With a full-time staff of nine, the Alliance works with regional teams. In Europe, for instance, three full-time staff coordinate more than fifty volunteers and interns.

Paul-Wandrille Parent came from France to spend three months as an intern with the Alliance beginning in July 2001. He spent his time in the U.N. library researching sustainable development. During his research, he discovered both the positive and the negative aspects of the concept.

"Sustainable development makes human beings responsible for the environment," Parent explains, "but the main difficulty is that the environment becomes more important than the human person."

He sees the work of the Alliance as important because it "can help the U.N. and other international organizations to focus on fundamental issues."

Another intern, Olivia Raw, saw her internship develop into a full-time job with the Alliance. Raw grew up in London and first met Halpine at a party in France in 2000.

"We were the only two native English speakers, so naturally we bonded," says Raw. In the end, the two traveled together by train back to Brussels. During the five-hour trip, Raw, who had been doing an internship at the European Commission, learned about the Alliance. "I was gripped by what I heard," Raw says.

Raw later spent two months living in New York, diving into documents, learning the U.N. language, and assisting at the World Summit on Children.

The International Catholic Youth Movement

The World Youth Alliance, begun in 1999 under the leadership of then-twenty-one-year-old Anna Halpine, encourages the United Nations and other international organizations to respect the dignity of the human person.

"I saw how delegates from the poorer countries were manipulated and how their words were twisted," says Raw. "An ideological imperialism was at hold in the U.N., and I experienced how member states were afraid to speak up about the inalienable dignity of each and every person."

Her time in New York was invaluable. "I was bathed in a culture of life," says Raw. "The ideas that the Alliance expressed were in my head, but no one had spelled them out in a language that was tangible for me as a young person."

In the end, Raw helped to set up the organization's European office, where she works as director of operations. The European staff represents more than eight hundred thousand European youth and has hosted conferences in Belgium, Spain, Italy, Portugal, France, Germany, Austria, Scotland, Luxembourg, Poland, and Slovakia.

While the group is not expressly religious, it draws from the writings of Pope John Paul II.

"He has to be recognized as one of the great philosophers of our time," says Halpine. "He is a great hero in my life.

"One of my favorite ideas is found in paragraph thirteen of Pope John Paul II's 1991 encyclical letter *Centissimus Annus* [On the Hundredth Anniversary of *Rerum Novarum*]," says Halpine. "When the Holy Father reflects on the cause for the collapse of Communism, he says that the collapse was not brought about by political or economic circumstances, but a faulty vision of the human person. Policies based on the wrong idea of the human person will ultimately fail. We try to bring that perspective to our work."

Halpine summarizes the organization's charter, saying, "The dignity of the human person begins at conception and is best nurtured in the family. Only through the family can we build a free and just society."

∞

Extraordinary Success

The World Youth Alliance has experienced success on several levels. Not only have they mobilized more than one million youth who support their vision of the dignity of the human person, but they have seen a handful of their young members move into elected office, and they have succeeded in affecting the language used in U.N. documents.

"Some of our ideas made it into the document on children that came out in 2002," says Halpine. "We've also worked to help keep some language out."

The International Catholic Youth Movement

In the fall of 2002, the Alliance helped shape the language being used in the European Parliament and at the Sixth Committee of the U.N. General Assembly regarding human cloning.

In a statement to the Economic and Social Council, Ambassador Sichan Siv reiterated the position that the international community should ban all human cloning. Included in his remarks was a reference to the position of the World Youth Alliance.

"To the youth, the future world leaders," said Ambassador Siv, "we hope that the Sixth Committee will be able to say, 'We heard you!'"

Ruse sees the value of the Alliance's work as part of a larger coalition of family-friendly nongovernmental organizations. "They are bringing young people together at international conferences [such as the World Children's Summit] to promote life and family," says Ruse.

Perhaps even more important is the interaction that is taking place at the personal level. Halpine recalled working with thirty young Africans at the Rio conference in Johannesburg in August 2002.

"There were two girls from very influential families — one Jewish and one Hindu," says Halpine. "The Hindu girl's family was very involved in Palestine, while the Jewish girl's family funded activities taking place in Israel. Yet, here were these two girls coming together to work upon shared values. The answers for these girls were clear, and they were working for a common cause. Encounters like that are very powerful.

"Our most lasting success," says Halpine, "has been to develop a language and an idea that is bringing together a generation. We are saying that this is who we see the human person as, and this is the kind of society that we want to create. It has been very exciting to see young people's willingness to come forward."

"Our success stems from the fact that we are embracing universal truths," says Halpine. "The Church embraces them because they are true also."

She finds working with the youth incredibly hopeful.

"People will sometimes say that it must be difficult to bring these ideas to the world, but our experience is opposite," says Halpine. "The world is hungry for these ideas, and the youth are eager to bring forward ideas that will build families and societies. The youth who are involved are giving up their lives for the purpose of doing something good for humanity and the world. I'm privileged to work with them. I'm witnessing people who will be the saints of the third millennium."

Clearly, young adults around the world are embracing the universal Church. The sheer numbers suggest that the Church of the future may very well be led by those in Africa, Asia, and Latin America. That has led some to speculate that future missionaries may one day embark from those continents to re-evangelize Europe and North America.

Events such as World Youth Day and organizations such as World Youth Alliance have helped to shrink the boundaries between countries and Catholics in those countries. Another way that those borders are collapsing is through modern communication media and the Internet.

∞

Their Life Is Wired

The Faith Online

"I learned much from the Internet, particularly from orthodox websites. After my 'discovery' of orthodox Catholicism, I began to find good material that was both positive and intelligent."

Paul Brzezinski, 32, billing clerk, Massapequa, New York

᪫

The influence of the Internet in today's Church can be seen in everything from youth-oriented Catholic websites and chat rooms to online Catholic singles organizations; from religious orders seeking vocations online to the rise of Catholic web logs and the "virtual parish."

According to a 2003 Pew Research Center survey, one-third of all Americans who are connected to the Internet use it to access religious and spiritual information. Between March 2000 and November 2002, the number of "religion surfers" doubled from eighteen million to thirty-five million.

An earlier Pew Center survey titled *CyberFaith: How Americans Pursue Religion Online,* reported that more than forty percent of surfers had used the Internet to send or receive prayer requests.

A study by analysts with the National Study of Youth and Religion also suggests that the web has become a significant place of religious connection for a sizable portion of religious teens in the United States. The study found that among teens who say that religious faith is "extremely important" to them, forty percent report using the Internet to visit religious websites a few times per month or more. Another twenty percent, who describe religious faith as "very important" to them, also say they visit religious sites a few times each month. According to author Tom Beaudoin,

Young and Catholic

Generation X represents approximately one-third of those active in cyberspace.[18]

The sheer amount of Catholic information available on the Internet is overwhelming. In less than two seconds, the average Internet user can utilize the Google search engine to locate nearly ten million Catholic web links.

With the advent of technologies such as Internet chat rooms and instant messaging, e-mail, cellular telephones, digital cameras, and peer-to-peer networks, young adults are able to communicate with one another twenty-four hours a day, seven days a week.

While some see such technologies as isolating, the vast majority of youth use them to stay connected. Faith-filled young adults use them to communicate with those who are like-minded. Much like World Youth Day, the Internet puts a universal face on the Catholic Church.

"You could certainly say that almost every Catholic organization has a website," says Br. John Raymond, co-founder of the Monks of Adoration and author of *Catholics on the Internet*. "Whatever was Catholic before, now has a website as part of its mission. It has outstripped television. Certainly, not every organization can be on TV."

"The only reason I own a television is because it hooks up to a VCR," admits Pete Vere, twenty-nine. "I would rather surf the Net than watch TV." An author and canon lawyer, Vere understands the importance of the Internet for Generation X. He served as a moderator on the youth website Onerock.com, a Catholic site by teens for teens.

"The Internet allows youth of a similar mind to get together," says Vere. "Onerock started because a group of youth was not

18 Beaudoin, *Virtual Faith*.

satisfied with the youth-oriented catechetical resources they were being offered. The materials were condescending and were trying to promote an agenda. Onerock allowed the teens to have real debate and meaty discussions."

Onerock is one of several popular Catholic youth-oriented websites that allow young adults to connect while providing a forum for social and doctrinal questions. Onerock's original founder, Martin Ford, graduated from high school and has moved on to college, but the site continues to be run by teens. It has spawned a web zine and a sizable message board, and has been featured on Vatican Radio.

The proliferation of Catholic websites, particularly those directed toward young adults, is staggering. One popular site aimed at youth is Life Teen's award-winning website. It receives an average of seven thousand page views per day and approximately twenty-three thousand unique visitors each month. Like most other sites, it features chat rooms, a place for teens to ask questions, and practical Church-related content. Another site, Omegarock.com is a web-based radio station that features contemporary Catholic music and information on the Faith. Phatmass.com has online forums for youth to talk about various topics, and Youthapostles.com is a Catholic chastity website for young adults featuring Cleveland, Ohio-based chastity educator and speaker Michele TePas. The site also features a monthly electronic magazine.

Twenty-three-year-old Stephanie Wood serves as coordinator of NextWaveFaithful.com, the youth division of the Family Life Center International and one of the most recent Catholic websites for youth. Geared for youth between the ages of sixteen and twenty-six, NextWaveFaithful.com is an online community where teens and young adults can participate in monitored chat rooms and discussion forums.

Young and Catholic

The outreach is geared for sixteen- to twenty-six-year-olds. "We're walking them through the transition years from teen to adulthood," says Wood. "At a youth ministry summit I attended in 2003, a Gallup poll researcher said that while younger teens are showing greater faithfulness and commitment to God, the biggest danger point is for eighteen- to twenty-nine-year-olds. They experience the greatest drop-off. We're trying to help that age group continue to make decisions for Christ and the Church.

"The young faithful are in pockets all over the country," says Wood, a 2003 theology graduate of Ave Maria College in Ypsilanti, Michigan. "We're trying to give them a place of support."

NextWaveFaithful.com features topic areas devoted to life, love, purpose, and truth. The site's name refers to the generation of the third millennium. It's also an allusion to surfing.

"A surfer knows that the third wave is the largest," says Wood. "I want this generation to rise up and make an impact on the world and the Church."

"They're discussing everything from dating to vocational discernment and Catholic apologetics," Wood says. "We're the online generation," she added. "Everyone is online. They log in every day to see what's happening."

Launched in December 2003, the site has logged an average of 750 youth visitors per day, and nearly twenty-six thousand per month.

"We have young people on the site from more than sixty foreign countries," says Wood. "Teens in India are talking to teens in New York. They love the sense of community and want to meet up with one other at World Youth Day 2005 in Cologne, Germany." Wood also hosts "The Wave Factor," the first Catholic teen weekly live call-in radio program on EWTN Global Catholic Radio.

Wood says that she is both concerned and hopeful about the future of the Church.

"Divorce statistics are very high. We don't have a lot going for us. The next generation is going to have a difficult time," Wood says. "I believe that we are living in an age of crisis. To say that we're not is to bury our head in the sand. We have our work cut out for us.

"Many of the young have been poorly catechized," she continues. "Many have no clear direction for their lives. Yet, I find them desperately searching for the truth. Many of the young who are entering adulthood clearly see the wasteland that has been left to us. Those who see it are willing to make a radical change because they don't want the same for themselves and their children. That is where the hope lies. They've witnessed the legacy of divorce and immorality and are deciding to accept a higher calling in their relationships, their faith, and their moral standards. There is a lot of commitment and faithfulness coming from this generation. Many will be more committed than their parents."

∞

Bridging the Generation Gap

The technology not only allows youth to connect with their peers, but it is also helping to bridge the gap between generations. Take, for example, Generation X computerphile and attorney Rachel Silverman, thirty, and Baby Boomer attorney David Wemhoff, forty-five. Although from different generations, the two South Bend, Indiana, attorneys collaborated to create the uniquely named youth-oriented site Groundpickle.com.

"Studies show that seventy-eight percent of Americans between the ages of twelve and seventeen use the Internet," says Wemhoff, "some using it as much as five hours per day."

Young and Catholic

With the help of University of Notre Dame law professor Charles Rice, Groundpickle.com was created to counter the kinds of misinformation offered by Planned Parenthood and the secular media. It offers resources to young men and women in crisis situations, including facts about abortion, contraception, peer pressure, sexually transmitted diseases, and drug use. The site also allows youth to compete for modest scholarships to continue their education.

"We developed a site where young men and women can come for straight talk on life-defining issues," explains Silverman. The site has received more than a hundred thousand visits since it first went live on March 13, 2003.

Catholic webmasters recognize this model of bringing "the truth to youth" through the Internet.

"Traditionally, the Catholic Church has been able to wait for people to come to church," says Paulist Fr. Brett Hoover, "but we realized that if we really cared about young people today, we'd have to go to them. The Internet was one of the places where we knew we would find them." As a result, the Paulists created the website BustedHalo.com as a way to reach young adults.

That recognition has also been made by Pope John Paul II. During his twenty-sixth World Communications Day message, the Holy Father spoke of the Internet as a new forum for proclaiming the gospel:

> For the Church, the new world of cyberspace is a summons to the great adventure of using its potential to proclaim the gospel message. . . . The Internet can offer magnificent opportunities for evangelization if used with competence and a clear awareness of its strengths and weaknesses. Above all, by providing information and stirring interest, it makes

possible an initial encounter with the Christian message, especially among the young who increasingly turn to the world of cyberspace as a window on the world.

It is clear, then, that while the Internet can never replace that profound experience of God which only the living, liturgical, and sacramental life of the Church can offer, it can certainly provide a unique supplement and support in both preparing for the encounter with Christ in community, and sustaining the new believer in the journey of faith which then begins.[19]

"Their life is wired," adds Br. Raymond. "They are media-oriented. While they cannot rely on the Internet for all aspects of their Faith, they can choose to use it in a faith-filled way." As an example, Br. Raymond points to the Monks of Adoration's eucharistic adoration chapel, which can be viewed over the Internet on a live web cam. The site, he says, is visited by more than a million visitors annually.

One of the pioneers in creating online Catholic content is Michael Galloway. Galloway started out working in the motion-picture and software industries and was instrumental in developing web-based email and data base technologies. In 1991, before the advent of the Internet and Yahoo, Galloway created Catholic Online. It originally existed as a bulletin board on Compuserve and operated through multiple servers located throughout Galloway's living room in California.

In 1994, Galloway became one of the first hundred people to purchase a web address and offer email addresses. Today, Catholic

[19] Pope John Paul II, "Internet — A New Forum for Proclaiming the Gospel": Message for 36th World Communications Day, May 12, 2002.

Online is run by a staff of twenty and is one of the most visited Catholic websites in the world, receiving upwards of a million unique visitors per day. When the organization launched a non-partisan political arm, Your Catholic Voice, in 2002, they registered more than two hundred thousand members in only six months.

Nearly two-thirds of Catholic Online's visitors, says Galloway, are between the ages of twenty-five and forty. Another fifteen percent are younger than twenty-five. The Internet, he says, is undoubtedly the medium of choice for the young.

"Youth don't like direct mail," says Galloway, "and diocesan newspapers are birdcage-liner for them. They use the Internet to communicate via email and instant messaging, they use it for news and information, and they use it to download material such as music. Kazaa, a peer-to-peer music source, receives as many as a hundred million hits every hour," says Galloway.

"We have seen a very definite upswing in youth going online, and visiting sites such as ours," he adds. "We just have to learn how to offer them something and distribute it to them."

To that end, Catholic Online has partnered with the Archdiocese of Cincinnati's youth ministry program to offer youth-oriented material through its Catholic Youth Online channel.

"Forty percent of our online information is on the lives of the saints," admits Galloway. "If there are two things the youth love, it's the Holy Father and the saints."

∽

Linking the World

One of the most ambitious online projects, the Online Catholic Encyclopedia at the New Advent website, was undertaken by Kevin Knight of Denver, Colorado, then twenty-six. Through the work of Knight and more than four hundred other volunteers from around the world, the entire set of the 1913 *Catholic Encyclopedia* has been transcribed and is available for search online. Begun nine years ago, the project was completed on May 1, 2000.

Pope John Paul II's visit to Denver during World Youth Day in August 1993 first inspired Knight to create the New Advent site.

"World Youth Day planted the seed of the New Advent apostolate," says Knight. "I wanted to create something that was unique and systematic, instead of producing a pamphlet here or an article there. I wanted people to see the vastness of the Catholic Church."

The New Advent website takes its name from the period leading up to the millennium, coined by John Paul II in his 1979 encyclical letter *Redemptor Hominis*. Archbishop J. Francis Stafford, then archbishop of Denver, first applied that term to the Blessed Mother and commissioned an icon of Our Lady of the New Advent as the patroness of Denver. This icon was very visible during World Youth Day.

Explains Knight, "New Advent is an all-encompassing Catholic website that ties together a variety of primary sources." In the autumn of 1995, he put St. Thomas Aquinas's *Summa Theologica* online. Soon afterward, Knight added works from the early Church Fathers. The *Catholic Encyclopedia* project began at the end of the year.

"The encyclopedia," says Knight, "demonstrates the collective power of people on the web. The project allowed people to participate in a common project, allowing us to do far more than any one of us could do individually."

Like medieval monks transcribing the Bible to make it available to others, hundreds of volunteers obtained copies of the original 1913 encyclopedia, often spending as much as an hour per page typing the articles into the computer, and then emailing them directly to Knight. Volunteers included people such as a retired medical doctor from New Mexico; a cloistered nun from Lufkin, Texas; and a graduate student and parish administrator from Maplewood, Minnesota.

"There were volunteers from all fifty states, as well as many foreign countries, including Canada, France, Germany, and Brazil," says Knight.

Based upon the responses Knight has received, the encyclopedia is being used by students, scholars, and others curious about the Faith from around the world. Tracking software reports that the website receives more than thirteen thousand visitors per day. "These include visitors from 150 countries," reports Knight.

The encyclopedia is also cropping up in both likely and unlikely places. Many of its entries are found in the Eternal Word Television Network online library archive files. In addition, notes Knight, "The anti-Catholic motion picture *Stigmata* included the web address for the Catholic Encyclopedia in the DVD liner notes," added Knight. "Many people who saw the movie wrote in with questions. Any link that can clear up misconceptions is a good thing.

"People stumble across the encyclopedia when they are searching for something tangential to the Church," explains Knight. "A search for medieval history, for example, might lead to you to it. Because of its scope and the ease of finding the encyclopedia's pages in searches, it tends to attract people. God uses it to attract people who are interested in the Church but don't realize it yet."

Br. John Raymond uses the encyclopedia in his own writing. Br. Raymond also used it to create a word game he uses as an instructional aid. He says that the online version is far more convenient than a version that sits on a bookshelf. "Catholic students, in particular, will find it useful," Br. Raymond says. "It is very thorough."

What is perhaps most startling is the effect the encyclopedia has had elsewhere in the world. ACI-PRENSA, a Catholic news-wire agency in South America and the most visited Catholic website in Spanish, undertook the task of translating the encyclo-pedia into Spanish on the eve of the new millennium. The agency used the same technique as Knight, enlisting the help of Spanish-speaking volunteers to transcribe the entire encyclopedia. They see the translation as their gift to the Church's effort to launch the New Evangelization.

Coordinator of the project, Giuliana Gerber of Peru, says that ACI-PRENSA was referred to the *Catholic Encyclopedia* by a bilin-gual U.S. user who is now a contributor to the translation. "Unfor-tunately, there was no Catholic encyclopedia in Spanish with the same approach and intellectual consistency as the English edition. Once we saw it, we said, 'This is it!' and launched the project," says Gerber.

Gerber explains that after ACI-PRENSA's first two years online, they kept getting requests from Catholics to solve common ques-tions about their Faith. "The *Catholic Encyclopedia* allows us to re-spond to all questions with one continuous effort," says Gerber.

Originally, ACI-PRENSA's effort included sixty volunteers, among them a mother in Uruguay, two Hispanic scholars from Ivy League universities in the United States, a pastor in Colombia, and others from Mexico, Argentina, and Spain. Today, ACI-PRENSA has more than ninety volunteers working to transcribe the encyclopedia.

The encyclopedia has also been used with success in places where the Church has been forced underground. This is especially true in Vietnam.

Vietnamese software engineer, An Dang, from Australia, assists Fr. John Tran Cong Nghi and his team of priests in maintaining

Young and Catholic

VietCatholic, a website for Vietnamese Catholics who now live all around the world after the communists took control of the country in 1975.

"The Vietnamese government," says Dang, "is still under communist rule. They hate Catholicism and have been trying to destroy the Church in Vietnam. They have put a lot of priests in prison. They try to control all aspects of the Church in Vietnam, including the Ordination of priests and bishops. Especially, they do not allow publication of any religious materials. No books, no magazines, no newspapers, no radio, no TV, and no Internet."

In an effort to aid the Church in Vietnam, Dang copies religious materials from the Internet onto CD-ROMs and sends them to priests in Vietnam, who then distribute the materials to the faithful.

Following the completion of the *Catholic Encyclopedia*, Dang felt that a CD-ROM version would be useful for those unable to access the Internet. He sought and obtained Knight's permission to produce a CD version. Weeks later Dang designed a special New Advent browser that helps users without Internet access browse and search a CD-ROM version of the encyclopedia.

In May 2000 a business associate successfully brought the CD to Saigon and trained several Vietnamese priests in its use.

"I have received many letters from priests and bishops saying that the *Catholic Encyclopedia* is a great resource. They remember all those who contributed to the *Catholic Encyclopedia* in their daily prayers," adds Dang.

Future plans include adding a "natural language" component to the site; this would allow users to ask questions such as, "Why do Catholics genuflect?" and return a specific, individual response. Explains Knight, "None of the questions being asked are new. They have all been asked before." Knight says he also hopes to be able to offer Catholic materials in Chinese. With a degree in Chinese language under his belt, he just might do it.

∞

Marriages Made in Cyberspace

Catholics are using the Internet to "connect" in more ways than one. Some Catholic singles are using it to find a spouse. Websites such as Ave Maria Singles, Catholic Singles, and St. Raphael Catholic Singles offer faith-filled resources that help match couples, showing that God can work through the Internet. All three of the services estimate that the majority of their users fall between the ages of twenty-five and forty.

Thirty-year-old Brian Barcaro started one of the largest, St. Raphael Catholic Singles, in 1998. The site currently has more than thirty thousand members. Far more than a dating service, St. Raphael hosts community forums that allow members to talk with one another on topics as diverse as apologetics and sports.

"We encourage activity beyond people just looking for others to date," says Barcaro. The forums have two effects: Catholic singles are able to make friends, and often those friendships develop into marriages.

Although smaller in numbers, Ave Maria Singles' statistics are still impressive. Its founder, Anthony Buono, estimates over eight thousand members, with some nine hundred in "serious courtships." So far, Ave Maria has led to more than 240 marriages and over a hundred engagements.

Ave Maria also has an innovative Ask Married Members forum, with topics dealing with everything from how to handle long-distance relationships to suggestions for activities on a first date.

Maria Kaczperski met her husband, Mark, using Ave Maria Singles.

Young and Catholic

When she first signed on to the service in February 1999, her expectations were pretty low. Her previous relationships had ended badly, and at age thirty-nine, she felt that time was running out. She certainly didn't hold out much hope for finding a date, much less a spouse, over the Internet.

"I didn't expect it to work out," she admits. In fact, she was convinced she'd be single for the rest of her life and had begun to make plans to work as a missionary in Honduras. "I certainly didn't think that God would use the Internet to have me meet my husband," she says.

In May, however, she began corresponding with Mark, a horticulture professor at Fort Valley State University in Macon, Georgia. In her profile, Maria wrote that she was going on a mission trip and needed prayer partners.

While Maria was serious about her faith, Mark wasn't an active Catholic at the time. Still, he agreed to pray for Maria and made the commitment to attend daily Mass for her. In fact, prior to her trip, he went back to the sacrament of Reconciliation for the first time in a long while.

Over the course of the next three months, the two emailed one another. "His letters were beautiful," Maria admits. In August, they agreed to meet one another for the first time at the Atlanta Botanical Gardens.

After that, they began talking to one another on the telephone more often and they began doing more together. Despite a two-and-a-half hour drive for Mark, they became very involved with the Young Adult Ministry offerings in Atlanta — Theology on Tap, Thank God It's First Fridays, the Songs of Solomon, and different Catholic apologetics seminars. Every morning at six, Mark would call Maria so that they could begin their day by praying the Rosary together.

In October, Mark first told Maria that he loved her. Maria was apprehensive at first, but then Mark wrote her a letter explaining what love meant to him.

"He described a type of sacrificial love," says Maria. "I had never been loved that way before." A month later, Maria told Mark that she loved him in return.

They were engaged on New Year's Eve and married on October 7, 2000 — the Feast of Our Lady of the Rosary. Today, they both work at the world's largest Catholic television network, the Eternal World Television Network in Irondale, Alabama.

Buono explained that one of the reasons online Catholic matchmaking works so well is that it eliminates the time people often spend simply trying to get to know one another through dating. Ave Maria, for example, asks detailed questions, allowing members to screen one another based upon questions not only of personality, but also regarding Catholic teaching on marriage, contraception, and abortion.

∞

Blogging for Christ

The young generation's desire for connectedness can further be witnessed in one of the more recent online trends, the advent of the "blog." Short for *web log*, a blog is a cross between a traditional website and an online diary. This form of personal journalism exploded among Catholics in late 2001 and early 2002, connecting communities of lay Catholics and religious around the world.

Web logs allows individuals or groups of users to post news, links, and commentary on an hourly, or even a minute-by-minute basis — free of charge and without the need to understand complex hyper-text markup language. The ease of the technology makes it possible for almost anyone to publish.

Young and Catholic

"It's impossible to keep up with them all, but we estimate that there are more than a million weblogs," says Evan Williams, CEO of Pyra Labs, the San Francisco–based company that designed the Blogger web-based software in the fall of 1999. "There are approximately fifteen hundred new weblogs created every day," he adds.

Early in 2002, two dozen self-identified Catholic blog sites existed. That number quickly escalated following a news story on Vatican Radio. Gerard Serafin's A Catholic Blog for Lovers now lists more than three hundred blogs with appropriate Catholic names such as Nota Bene, Annunciations, and Gregorian Rant.

In addition to the attention from Vatican Radio and traditional secular media sources, many feel that the clergy sexual-abuse scandal was a primary factor contributing to the increase in Catholic blogs.

"People are feeling a lot of strong emotion about the clerical sexual-abuse scandal, and people want to speak up," says Catholic "blogger" Peter Nixon, of Concord, California. He oversees the Catholic blog site Sursum Corda.

Kathy Shaidle, of Toronto, Ontario, is one of the Catholic blog pioneers. She started her site, Relapsed Catholic, in 2000. She says that she witnessed a thirty percent increase in the number of visitors to her site when the clergy sexual-abuse stories broke. "I've been told that I've inspired others to take up blogging, to express their thoughts on the scandal," adds Shaidle.

Beyond the scandal, however, individuals find distinct ways to use their blogs. Some use them to advance their work. Kathryn Lively, of Come On, Get Lively, uses her blog to highlight publishing projects of her FrancisIsidore Electronic Press. Amy Welborn uses her blog, Open Book, to promote her books and work out writing ideas. Canonist Pete Vere uses his site, Clog, to address reader's canonical concerns.

"In a time when the Church is experiencing a shortage of canonists, blogging allows me to interact with average Catholics and address their concerns pertaining to canon law. It allows me to clarify certain rights Catholics have within the Church, correct misconceptions, and show the faithful they have nothing to fear from canon law," says Vere.

Others, such as Tom Kreitzberg of Silver Spring, Maryland, use their blogs to offer political or social commentary. Kreitzberg quotes P. G. Wodehouse, who says that "people become authors when their hopes of getting letters to the editor published are frustrated." This explains the motivation behind Kreitzberg's own blog, Praying the Post.

"There are people who blog to promote themselves professionally; there are people who blog to promote themselves personally; there are people who blog to promote their ideas or perspectives," adds Kreitzberg.

Mainstream media and news organizations have not only begun quoting blogs, but they have also created blogs of their own. Religious periodicals such as *Christianity Today*, *Touchstone*, and *National Review*, and even apostolates now maintain blogs.

Many feel that bloggers are building a virtual Christian community — one that Catholic bloggers themselves have taken to calling "St. Blog's Parish." Like voices are finding one another.

"What a blessing and inspiration Catholic blogging has been," exclaims Jeanine Webb, a seventy-year-old grandmother from Eugene, Oregon. "Eugene is the capital of alternative-lifestyle types, so it's been reassuring to be able to read and communicate with faith-filled, active, intelligent people of my Faith. It's helped me to be more active too," says Webb, who, after reading a suggestion from a web log, decided to call her local parish to schedule a prayer vigil.

Young and Catholic

Tara Conway, a communications consultant in Washington, D.C., concedes that reading others' blogs has helped her to feel as if she knows them. "I can foresee the day when bloggers might well hold mini-conferences just to get together to meet one another and talk in person," adds Conway.

The virtual community sometimes becomes an actual community, spurring collective action. In October 2003, Catholic bloggers united to bring attention to the plight of Terri Schindler-Schiavo, a disabled woman in Pinellas Park, Florida, whom the Florida courts had ruled could be starved to death. In part, due to the attention paid to the case by various Catholic blogs, a large number of readers put pressure on the Florida legislature and Governor Jeb Bush to pass "Terri's Law." Governor Bush gave an executive order to have Schiavo's feeding tube reinserted. The blogging community also organized a charitable collection to send fellow blogger Fr. Rob Johansen to Florida to provide spiritual care for Schiavo and her family.

"Surfing the Catholic blogs has done wonders to restore my joy and hope," says Barbara Nicolosi, executive director of the Christian screenwriting organization Act One: Writing for Hollywood. Nicolosi operates the blog Church of the Masses.

"In an age in which clinging to 'organized religion' is popularly reckoned to be for the brain-dead, St. Blog's Parish has reminded me how smart our Faith is. The ultimate source of lasting community is when people cleave together to the same truth."

Young Catholics are using the Internet to deepen their faith in numerous ways. Blogs offer a place for converts to share their journey with others. Instant messaging allows young people to discuss ideas with friends who are several states, or countries, away. Still others are using the technology to meet and to fall in love. Some are using the Internet to help them discern their vocation.

The Faith Online

The impact of the Internet cannot be denied. It has eliminated pre-existing borders and is allowing the universal Church to interact in ways that were never possible before. As technologies advance, it will continue to play a significant role in the Church of the future.

∞

With Clarity and Authority

A New Generation Answers the Vocational Call

*"When it comes to our faith, it's all
or nothing. There is no halfway Catholic.
You should have a joy about that."*

Bobby Garrison, 19, seminarian, Atlanta, Georgia

With reality television programs all the rage, thirty-one-year-old Kevin Wright of Littleton, Colorado, figured if you can't beat them, join them.

In 2002, Wright traveled with a camera crew and a group of thirty-three young adults as they made their way on a two-week religious pilgrimage through France and Italy. The footage ultimately became "Onward Pilgrims," a reality television program that aired on EWTN.

"On day two, you had people who admitted that they were struggling with the Faith," says Wright, "but by day fourteen, many of the pilgrims spoke about how their lives had changed. There is no stronger evangelistic tool than a pilgrimage. The series showed that."

Young adults serious about their faith display a heightened receptivity to the importance of their vocation, whether it's a vocation to the single state, or married or religious life. Naturally, they wonder what God is asking of them and what they are to do with their lives.

For Diana Jelski, a thirty-year-old youth minister with Our Mother of Good Counsel Catholic Church in Philadelphia, "Onward Pilgrims" was an opportunity to explore her vocation. She thought she had a vocation to religious life, but the pilgrimage led her to discover a different vocation.

Young and Catholic

A lifelong Catholic, after high school Jelski turned her back on the Church for a time. Later she attended Immaculata University in Philadelphia.

"As I studied theology, there were things I learned that I wished I had known when I was younger," says Jelski. "Through my studies, I became stronger in my faith." After graduating from college, she decided to go on a pilgrimage.

"I had considered the religious life and went with the intention of praying for my vocation," says Jelski. "I was trying to discern where God was taking me."

While on the pilgrimage, Fr. Mariche Koch, with the Franciscan Friars of Renewal, sat Jelski down and told her, "It's time to search for your vocation."

Jelski spent a lot of time praying at the various shrines she visited, and talking with others. "Traveling with the other pilgrims and visiting the holy sites helped me to find peace for when God finally said, 'Here it is,' " she says.

After their return home, Fr. Koch invited the pilgrims to join him on an additional pilgrimage, a four-day hike from New Jersey to Our Lady of Czestochowa in Doylestown, Pennsylvania. It was on that pilgrimage that Jelski's vocation suddenly became clear.

During that pilgrimage, Jelski met a young man from Brooklyn named Jan. "Fr. Koch introduced us during a water break," recalls Jelski, "and we spent the rest of the weekend talking. I wondered whether this man was my vocation or a stumbling block."

It was while Jelski was later visiting the Daughters of St. Paul that she realized her true vocation, and Jan realized that he didn't want her to be a nun. Jan proposed on the feast of the Holy Family, and they were married on June 1, 2002.

"I had to go to Europe and all the way back to find my vocation," says Jelski.

"We credit Our Lady for bringing us together," she says. The couple traveled to Rome for their honeymoon, receiving a papal blessing from the Holy Father. The couple lost their first child, Francis Michael, and buried him at Our Lady of Czestochowa.

"Our faith is fundamental," adds Jelski. "We can't imagine who we would be without our faith life. It's helped us through everything . . . living in separate states, and losing our first child."

Recognizing the need for young Catholics to meet one another, Wright created Catholic Adventures — a travel company offering pilgrimages and cruises for those in their twenties and thirties.

"I'm trying to capture those who feel alienated," says Wright. "It's harder for young adults to fit into their parishes. I'm working to bring these people together."

Bringing people together and helping them to recognize their baptismal call is the work of the Colorado Springs–based Catherine of Siena Institute.

∞

Creating a Culture of Discernment

Sherry Weddell, codirector of the Catherine of Siena Institute, doesn't believe that the Church has a vocations crisis. Rather, she believes that it is facing a "crisis of vocation" because it has not adequately prepared Catholics to understand the word and its meaning in people's lives.

"We still think that the word *vocation* means 'ecclesial vocation,' " says Weddell. "If you don't have a call to religious life, we ignore you."

Weddell is trying to change that, using teaching teams to help create a "culture of discernment." The goal of the institute is to make local parishes places where all baptized persons — especially adults — are challenged to be disciples, are given formation, and are empowered to discern God's call and answer it. They have had a tremendous response to their Called and Gifted seminars, particularly among young adults in places such as San Francisco, the Twin Cities, and Denver.

"Young adults have an enormous hunger," says Weddell. "They are seeking to understand the significance and importance of their life. Our workshops help move them from vague seekers, into someone who has been called and prepared by God for a history-changing life in some way. This gives young adults hope."

Weddell points to the success of a program in Seattle alone, where they offered a parish-based initial discernment program that involved everyone in the parish for monthly meetings.

"From 650 families, we had eight people enter religious life in two years," says Weddell.

That discernment, however, says Weddell, is helpful not only for those discerning religious life, but also for those discerning a lay vocation. She provided the example of Scott Moyer in San Francisco, who felt drawn to build a Christian community, but because he didn't feel called to be a priest, he didn't think it was possible.

"I felt that a part of me was never going to live," Moyer told Weddell.

Following the Institute's Called and Gifted workshop, Moyer realized that answering his call was possible outside of the priesthood. As a result, he changed careers and is now the director of adult faith formation at St. Dominic's parish in San Francisco and is pursuing a master's degree in theology at the Dominican School of Philosophy and Theology in Berkeley, California.

"His entire life has been turned upside down," says Weddell. "We hear these stories all the time."

A New Generation Answers the Vocational Call

⚭

You Shall Know Them by Their Fruits

Virtually every apostolate, movement, and organization mentioned in the previous chapters of this book has generated vocations as a result of its work.

The Kansas City Young Adults have produced at least three seminarians: Greg Hammes, Matt Cushing, and Matt Hauschild. The Newman Foundation at the University of Illinois, Champaign-Urbana continues to produce between ten and fifteen religious vocations annually through its programs. Approximately thirty young people who have participated in Youth for the Third Millennium missions are discerning ecclesial vocations. At Benedictine College, during the 2002-2003 school year alone, nine graduates went on to pursue a religious vocation. Twelve percent of Thomas Aquinas College's graduates have pursued a vocation. Fifteen percent of NET team members have gone on to pursue a vocation, and more than three hundred former Life Teen participants have entered the seminary or are considering religious life.

"Those campus ministers who have made a concerted effort to promote religious vocations to Catholic college students are experiencing tremendous success," says Ed Franchi, executive director of the Cincinnati-based Catholic Campus Ministry Association. "It's not unusual for them to have several students entering seminary per year."

⚭

A New Breed of Priests

"These priests are a very different breed from their fathers and grandfathers," says Weddell.

They include priests such as Fr. Patrick Winslow, thirty-five, parochial vicar of St. Vincent de Paul in Charlotte, North Carolina.

Not only does Fr. Winslow serve his flock, but he also volunteers his time to provide weekly audiotaped lectures and lecture notes via the Internet for more than seventy Catholic Scripture study groups around the country. Launched in September 2003, the study groups vary in size from thirty participants to three hundred. At St. Vincent de Paul, more than 275 people participate weekly.

Fr. Winslow credits his father for the idea.

"He used to do something similar as a volunteer in prisons," he says.

Fr. Winslow sees the Scripture study work as an integral part of his priesthood. He says that his vocation has been shaped by the generation he grew up in as well as by his seminary education.

"I've never known the Church to stop changing," says Fr. Winslow. "I remember it being one way in the 1970s, another in the 1980s, and another in the 1990s. For priests of my generation, at a certain level, we don't want the Church to change any more.

"In my generation you find a great desire to learn the teachings of the Church and not anyone's hybridization or alteration of them," he explains. "That comes from our unique time in history where people can find anyone teaching anything that they want to hear. Young priests are responding to the clarity and the authority of Christ in the Church, which stands in contrast to the complete din and cacophony of the voices of the world.

"The Faith, clearly presented, breeds vocations," adds Fr. Winslow. "It has been my experience that those dioceses which are speaking clearly about the Faith — which is countercultural — are getting vocations."

"Vatican II was not springtime for the Church; it was autumn," said the late Fr. Ronald Lawler, author of *Catholic Sexual Ethics*, quoting the late Cardinal John J. Wright. "The purpose of the council was to gather into the barn seed for the time when the winter ends. Pope John Paul II said that the end of the Jubilee was the end of the winter. We're on the way to spring, but it doesn't come suddenly."

Many young priests today share Fr. Lawler's belief that a new springtime is on the way. In particular, Lawler has observed that young priests are increasingly supportive of Natural Family Planning (NFP).

"Of priests ordained over the past ten to twelve years, nearly one hundred percent of them support NFP," said Lawler. "They know what life is all about, and they have a strong morality rooted in love."

It's a trend that has been observed by others as well. Sociologist and liberal-leaning priest Fr. Andrew Greeley, writing in *The Atlantic Monthly*, notes that, "a generation of conservative young priests is on the rise in the U.S. Church. These are newly ordained men who . . . define themselves in direct opposition to the liberal priests who came of age in the 1960s and 1970s."[20]

Citing sociologist Dean R. Hoge's 2002 study, *The First Five Years of the Priesthood: A Study of Newly Ordained Catholic Priests,* Greeley observes that young priests tend to support the celibate priesthood and to respect the Church's teaching regarding the ordination of women.

"Younger priests," Fr. Greeley wrote, "are more than twice as likely as priests aged fifty-five to sixty-five to think that birth control and masturbation are always wrong, and they are significantly more likely to think that homosexual sex and premarital sex are always wrong."

[20] Andrew Greeley, "Young Fogeys," *The Atlantic Monthly* (January/February 2004).

Young and Catholic

Fr. George Welzbacher, pastor of St. Agnes Catholic Church in St. Paul, Minnesota, says that in some dioceses — such as St. Paul-Minneapolis — the percentage of young priests who reject the dissenters' agenda constitutes a "massive majority." Fr. Welzbacher serves as pastor of the Church that has produced the greatest number of St. Paul-Minneapolis's priests.

Efforts by some priests in dioceses such as Milwaukee, New Ulm, St. Cloud, and St. Paul-Minneapolis, calling for discussions about the propriety of abolishing mandatory celibacy, have not been supported by younger priests. In nearly every case, the letters have contained few, if any, priests under the age of forty-five.

"For the great majority of America's younger priests, the Magisterium is no longer the enemy. What they have signed up for is the authentic Roman Catholic Church," says Fr. Welzbacher.

Many of the younger priests credit Pope John Paul II for their attraction to a priestly vocation. He is the only pontiff they have ever known, and consequently they are devoted to his vision for the Church.

"I was twelve when Karol Wojtyla was made Pope," says Fr. James Capoverdi, who has been a priest with the Diocese of Providence, Rhode Island, for eight years. "All during my teens, I was impressed by his vigor in trying to turn the Culture of Death. He inspired me to try to be holy and orthodox. Our Church has known both sinners and saints as popes. We're fortunate to have such a Vicar of Christ [as John Paul II] in the Chair of St. Peter."

Fr. Capoverdi, who first felt called to the priesthood at the age of nine, concelebrated with the Holy Father at World Youth Day in Toronto. He attended the event with a group of thirty youth from the Providence area.

Atlanta seminarian Bobby Garrison, who also attended World Youth Day in Toronto, echoes Fr. Capoverdi's comments.

A New Generation Answers the Vocational Call

"The first time I saw the Pope, I became teary-eyed because of all the wonderful work he's done for the Church, and knowing all he's been through and the faithful shepherd he has been," says Garrison. "In his weakened condition he came all the way here to see us. That shows his love for us."

Garrison adds that the priestly sexual-abuse scandals haven't discouraged his religious vocation. He compared them to the September 11, 2001 attacks.

"When your country is attacked, it makes you want to defend it," Garrison explains. "The scandals have made me want to fight for our Church. God allows evil so that greater good can come from it."

At the papal welcoming ceremony in Toronto, John Paul II told those gathered, "We see what happens when hatred, sin, and death take command. To follow Jesus — it means rejecting the lure of sin no matter how attractive it may be. Young people listening to me, answer the world with strong and generous hearts. He is counting on you. Never forget, Christ needs your youth and general enthusiasm to be salt and light in the new millennium. Answer His call by placing your lives in His service. Trust Christ, because He trusts in you. John Paul II loves you all."

"In fifteen years, when those from the 1960s generation of priests are deceased or retired and the numbers have hit bottom and start to grow again, the ones who will remain will be youngish and orthodox," predicts Weddell. "That's when we'll see the real fruits of the Second Vatican Council, as the John Paul II generation, steeped in the genuine teaching of the council and tested by opposition and scandal, move into major power and influence." The change, she notes, is already beginning.

That change can be seen in the numbers of U.S. seminarians. The number of diocesan seminarians has increased fourteen percent since the late 1990s. Seminarians in religious orders have also increased over that period. For some communities, such as the Western Dominican Province, as much as a third of their community is currently in formation. Although the increases aren't high enough to replace priests lost through death and retirement, the numbers tell a positive story about vocations to the priesthood.

The success of ecclesial vocations can most clearly be witnessed through those dioceses and seminaries that are attracting vocations. Those that are receiving the greatest number of vocations include Mount St. Mary's in Emmitsburg, Maryland; the Pontifical College Josephinum in Columbus, Ohio; and Mount Angel Seminary in St. Benedict, Oregon. The dioceses that are attracting young men include Arlington, Virginia; Atlanta; Denver; Peoria and Rockford, Illinois; Kansas City, Kansas; Fall River, Massachusetts; Newark, New Jersey; Bridgeport, Connecticut; Charlotte, North Carolina; Lansing, Michigan; Lincoln and Omaha, Nebraska; and Wichita, Kansas, just to name a few.

In his controversial 2002 book *Goodbye! Good Men*, author Michael Rose points to the Diocese of Lincoln, Nebraska, and the Archdiocese of Denver as two that are experiencing a marked rise in vocations.

Lincoln, Rose notes, had forty-four seminarians when its Seminary of St. Gregory the Great opened in August 1998.

"The relatively small Diocese of Lincoln," Rose writes, "has consistently had one of the highest rates of Ordination in the country over the past several decades and has never experienced a shortage of priests."[21]

---

[21] Michael Rose, *Goodbye! Good Men: How Catholic Seminaries Turned Away Two Generations of Vocations from the Priesthood* (Cincinnati: Aquinas Publishing), 346.

Likewise, Rose cites the statistics for Denver, where vocations have increased from twenty-six seminarians in 1991 to sixty-eight in 1999, plus an additional twenty studying for religious orders.[22] "If you're a young person looking for a diocese, you're going to look where there are young men," says Stella Marie Jeffrey. "It's not just the priesthood, but it's your brotherhood, too." Jeffrey's diocese of Fargo counts sixty priests ordained after 1992. Fifty percent of the diocese's active priests have been ordained less than ten years. "We have very young priests. I'm excited about what God is doing here," Jeffrey adds.

∞

Kansas Turnaround

One archdiocese that has seen a dramatic turnaround in vocations is that of Kansas City, Kansas. In the past nine years, the archdiocese has witnessed a sevenfold increase in its number of seminarians.

"When Archbishop James Keleher was appointed in 1993, we had only three men in seminary," recalls Fr. Brian Schieber, director of vocations for the archdiocese. "Archbishop Keleher said that his number-one priority would be vocations. In 2002 we had twenty-three seminarians. We'll be ordaining nine men over the next two years."

Fr. Schieber attributes the increase to a variety of efforts. He cites as key examples the support of the bishop, the spread of perpetual eucharistic adoration — particularly among suburban parishes — the work of the archdiocese's four Serra clubs, and the popular young-adult programs in Kansas City, at Benedictine College and at the University of Kansas.

[22] Ibid., 347.

Young and Catholic

"The Kansas City young-adult group has about 270 members who gather weekly for a holy hour, Bible studies, Mass, and dinner," Fr. Schieber explains. "Three of this year's new seminarians came from that group.

"We're blessed that I am able to work as vocations director full time," adds Fr. Schieber. "Many dioceses have vocations directors whose time is divided between parish work."

Archbishop Keleher's support has also been key to the success, he says, noting that the archbishop pays personal attention to vocations.

"Last January the bishop led a vocations retreat," Fr. Schieber explains. "During that retreat, he spent time individually speaking with each of the twenty-seven young men. Three of them entered seminary this fall."

Aside from the success of particular diocesan seminaries, nontraditional vocational discernment is also producing many religious vocations. One popular discernment program that is feeding several dioceses is the Pre-Theologate, founded at Franciscan University of Steubenville.

∞

Called to the Priesthood
Joseph Williams entered Franciscan University of Steubenville in the fall of 1996 after receiving his pre-med bachelor's degree from the University of Minnesota. He had every intention of following in his father's footsteps — the field of medicine. Instead, he ended up following in another Father's footsteps.

Fr. Joseph Williams is but one of fifty-eight priests who have emerged from the Pre-Theologate.

"Within weeks of being at Steubenville, I learned of the program," explains Fr. Williams. "Fr. David Testa, then director of the program, told me that if I had even an inkling toward the priest-hood, amidst the chaos and false promises of contemporary culture, there was a good chance that God might indeed be calling me to the priesthood," he recalls. "He also assured me that God is never outdone in generosity, and that if I gave this time to the Lord, it would bear fruit in whatever vocation I pursued in the future."

That began Williams's year and a half in the program as preparation for major seminary in St. Paul and his Ordination in May 2002. Fr. Williams now serves as parochial vicar at the Cathedral of St. Paul in St. Paul, Minnesota.

The program takes seriously the United States Conference of Catholic Bishops' June 2000 statement encouraging new approaches to fostering vocations. "We need to look at new ways to help create an environment in which someone can say yes to religious life or the priesthood," that statement declares.

The program allows young men the opportunity to study philosophy and theology on a coed campus, while learning about the lifestyle of a priest. Not only does it provide young men the freedom to discern a vocation, but it also allows them to take courses on a regular college campus while doing those things that other college students do — pursuing a degree, making friends, and in the program's first two years, even dating.

The young men who are accepted into the Pre-Theologate program live in the same college residence with the priest-director of the program. In the residence is a chapel, where they attend daily Mass. In the context of the program, they learn about the life of a priest by living it: they pray the Liturgy of the Hours, study Catholic thought, and develop solidarity with one other.

This formation leads the students to deep involvement in the Liturgy of the Church in the context of commitment to communal prayer, individual spiritual direction, a communal life of brother-hood, and fidelity to studies. Discerning and preparing for the priest-hood while receiving a liberal-arts education, the student achieves a broad knowledge of that humanity he hopes to evangelize.

The Pre-Theologate program allows men to nurture their vo-cations in a college setting, without having to take the more drastic step of entering a seminary. While they discern their voca-tions — and fulfill all the requirements for entrance into a major seminary, should they so choose — they're also working toward their academic degrees.

Participants also credit the program's structure as one of its strengths. "What is exceptional about the program is that it has a collegiate feel without losing the structure of prayer and fraternal community. The program holds that tension quite well," says Fr. Williams, a 1998 graduate of the program.

It is not only college-age men who are attracted to the pro-gram. Older men participate as well. John Klockeman left a career in the aerospace industry in the early 1990s when he felt a calling to the priesthood. He was accepted into the Pre-Theologate pro-gram at Franciscan University of Steubenville.

Klockeman describes his three years in the program as "the most beautiful years of my life. The Pre-Theologate helped me shore up what was missing in my religious education and gave me a good foundation. It prepared me to be a priest of the third millen-nium." Ordained in May 2000, Father Klockeman serves as associ-ate pastor at St. Olaf Catholic Church in downtown Minneapolis.

Fr. Tom Holloway, pastor of St. Mary's in Pontiac, Illinois, says the key to the program is prayer. "Fr. Augustine Donegan, TOR, impressed on us the paramount importance of daily prayer before the Blessed Sacrament, as well as daily meditation on God's word," he says. " 'My prayer for you,' he would say, 'is that if you pass a single day in which you eat and satisfy yourself but neglect to spend time being fed by the Lord Jesus, may you become sick as a dog! And if you go to bed having neglected the Scriptures, may you not be able to sleep a wink!' "

Fr. Cody describes the men as "prayer warriors" who enter into a community life that "captures their youthful zeal, enthusiasm, and passion for Jesus."

The program traces its beginnings to a group of seven men thinking about the priesthood who gathered at Franciscan University of Steubenville in 1985. That group met regularly at the campus's Holy Spirit Friary with a friar as their guide. From that group came four diocesan priests, a Dominican, a Franciscan, and a Trappist. Eventually, the group was recognized as one of the university's approximately forty "households" — small groups of prayerful friendship and support.

It wasn't until ten years later, in 1995, that the program became formalized when the late Fr. David Testa was hired as full-time director. For the next five years, the program experienced strong growth and eventually split into three separate households — *Living Stones* for freshmen and sophomores, *Koinonia* for juniors and seniors, and *Electi Mariae* for nontraditional students.

The program jumped from a household of twenty men to three households totaling eighty. During 2004 it numbered nearly one hundred.

"To date, the program has led to fifty-eight priests, seventy percent of them diocesan," says Fr. John Cody, current director of the program at Steubenville.

As the program grew, so did the need to raise money for scholarships. "Young men often graduate with large student loans," explains Carpenter, "and seminaries do not want to take on students with loans." Therefore, Carpenter worked with Fr. Testa to raise scholarship dollars. "We were raising about a quarter of a million dollars per year when we left Steubenville," says Carpenter.

When the Pre-Theologate program had reached its natural capacity at Steubenville, with men's names on a waiting list, Fr. Testa wondered if the program would work in a new setting. He recruited three students to accompany him, and together they launched a similar program at Ave Maria College in the fall of 2000. Fr. Patrick Egan succeeded Fr. Testa following his death from cancer in June 2002.

As a testament to the Pre-Theologate program's strength, it has even earned praise from those students who end up discerning that a religious vocation is not for them. Steubenville Pre-Theologate student Jon Ferguson says, "Every semester I have been in the program, at least one guy has left. Not one of them has ever regretted joining."

Tim DelCastillo is a prime example. A 2001 graduate of the program, DelCastillo discerned that his call was not to the ministerial priesthood.

"I am grateful for the formation that the program provided me in my spiritual life, training in manhood, and a greater understanding and appreciation of the vocation of the priesthood and religious life," says DelCastillo. "As one being called to the vocation of marriage, the program was very beneficial for me in my discernment. It was through trying to live out the life a priest, to a limited degree, that I was able to discover that this was not the vocation that God was calling me to."

Fr. Cody agrees. "Whether they become priests or not, I see the program as a win-win for the Church," he adds. "Most men are undeveloped in their emotional life and therefore don't know how to be good husbands and fathers. Never before in my life have I seen men able to communicate on every level as do the men in this program. I'm convinced that those men who decide to leave the program will be better husbands and fathers. They appreciate the gift of manhood, and they will be better able to contribute to their community and the Church."

"The Pre-Theologate is about building your life together as a community," adds Fr. Cody. "The men come seeking the will of the Lord in their life. At seminaries, in general, the vehicle for conversion is rules and regulations. By contrast, in the Pre-Theologate, the conversion is from the inside out. Aside from the obligation to pray, we have very few rules. The men are the formators of each other. There is a positive peer pressure for the men to develop a personal relationship with Jesus Christ through a regimen of prayer and silence."

The program has even attracted the attention of several bishops, including Archbishop Michael Sheehan of Santa Fe; Newark Archbishop John Myers; Archbishop James Keleher of Kansas City; Bishop Joseph Kurtz of Knoxville; and Anthony Cardinal Bevilaqua of the Archdiocese of Philadelphia. One bishop, Robert Carlson, of Sioux Falls, has served as a retreat master for men in the Pre-Theologate program.

"Only a short visit will tell you this is a real jewel and something that will benefit any diocese," Bishop Robert Carlson says of the program.

Several dioceses are sending men to the Pre-Theologate rather than to a traditional seminary. These include Bridgeport, Connecticut; Manchester, New Hampshire; Fall River, Massachusetts; Atlanta and Savannah, Georgia; Sioux Falls, South Dakota; Omaha, Nebraska; and Santa Fe, New Mexico. The archdioceses of Washington, D.C., and Baltimore, Maryland, are also considering the program. "We've had seventeen men from different dioceses in 2002, with at least another four coming in 2003," says Fr. Cody.

"I credit the increase in the number of seminarians for the Diocese of Steubenville at least in part to the program," says Bishop-Emeritus Gilbert I. Sheldon of the Diocese of Steubenville, Ohio. "I believe if something similar were implemented at other Catholic colleges and universities, it would go a long way toward alleviating the present shortage of vocations to the priesthood."

The growth trend in religious vocations is also observable in the numbers of young adults being attracted to nondiocesan religious orders such as Boston's Brothers of Hope; the Legionaries of Christ; New York's Sisters of Life; the Nashville Dominicans; the Franciscan Friars of the Renewal; the Franciscan Sisters of the Sorrowful Mother; the Poor Clare Nuns of Perpetual Adoration; the Sisters of Mary, Mother of the Eucharist; Chicago's Society of St. John Cantius; and the Western Dominican Province, among others. The stories of these thriving new orders still remain largely untold. Some have been so successful in so few years that they lack the space to house all of their new aspirants.

∞

Manhattan's Oasis of Peace

Sacred Heart Convent is an oasis of peace and quiet amid the activity and noise of midtown Manhattan. There is no television, no stereo, no clock radio, and no Internet access. Operated by the Sisters of Life, the convent provides a home not only for eleven sisters who live there, but also for women who find themselves in crisis pregnancies.

"We think of Sacred Heart as a holy respite," says Mother Agnes Mary Donovan, the order's superior general.

John Cardinal O'Connor first speculated on the need for such an order in his November 2, 1989 column for the New York archdiocesan newspaper. That column, titled "Help Wanted: Sisters of Life," was widely reported in both the secular and religious press. At the end of October 1990, O'Connor conducted a discernment retreat for inquirers. On June 1, 1991, eight women, including Sr. Agnes, were received as postulants in the Pious Association of the Sisters of Life. The order has grown to include thirty-two sisters, seven postulants, and seven novices in all.

The order is dedicated to the protection and enhancement of the sacredness of human life, and to this end, the sisters profess not only the vows of poverty, chastity, and obedience, but also a fourth vow to protect and advance the sacredness of human life.

The sisters provide a variety of services in their efforts for life. Since their creation, they have been doing the work of evangelization at Our Lady of New York in the Bronx, going on the road to explain the Church's teaching on human life and love.

"We go wherever we are invited," explains Mother Agnes.

In 1994, the sisters began doing retreat work. This includes retreats for those working in the pro-life movement, as well as retreats of prayer and healing for those suffering from the consequences of having had an abortion.

Sacred Heart Convent officially opened on June 28, 1999. Its mission is to serve women in difficult pregnancies and local mothers in need of baby supplies such as food, formula, and diapers. Their first guest arrived on their doorstep before the convent was ready.

"She came on December 26, 1997 and we knew that this was God at work," recalls Mother Agnes. "So she lived among the painting with the rest of us."

"This woman felt as if she were in an impossible situation," explains Mother Agnes. "Although she would describe herself as pro-choice, she didn't feel abortion was an option for her. When she realized she was pregnant, she threw herself on her bed and begged God to help her. She said, 'I will give you one year of my life, so that this child might have life, but I want my life back.' She stayed with us for a year and ended up giving her baby up for adoption. A year later, she came back to celebrate with us, and she commented that God had given her life back to her, and it was much better. That is the truth of every woman who has stayed here. They find themselves better people for having been here."

The convent is unique in that the sisters share the home with the women. Each woman has a private room of her own, but they share a common living and dining room. The women are invited to take part in the prayer life of the sisters, and the Mass. Some take part; others do not. In 2003 alone, the sisters served more than seven hundred pregnant women in New York.

"The women, even if they are not able to pray in their own lives, know that we are praying for them all day long. The bells call us to prayer and meals. We begin each day at five a.m. with prayer, and end each day in prayer," explains Mother Agnes.

This living side-by-side benefits both the women and the sisters. "This is a beautiful work," Mother Agnes says. "It allows us to become holy."

She compares it to having guests in your home.

"In life outside the convent," she laughs, "after about five days we're ready for guests to go home. However, these women come to stay with us for a year. So every day we have guests in our home whom we love. It gives us the opportunity to love others as God loves: unconditionally. They are a great gift to us.

"The women who stay with us inevitably tell us, after being here a while, that it feels safe," Mother Agnes continues. "At first I thought they meant that they felt safe in New York. Now I realize that they mean safe in an emotional and spiritual sense."

A New Generation Answers the Vocational Call

The pro-life network of the Church, pro-life groups, and crisis-pregnancy centers across the country refer women to the convent. "We never have an empty room," explains Mother Agnes. "If New York had thirty homes like this, they would all be full. There is a great, great need for this work."

Mother Agnes says it was nothing less than a "direct hit from God" that motivated her to join the order nine years ago, at age thirty-nine. At the time, she was working as a professor at Columbia University.

"On an annual retreat, I experienced the love of God in a way in which I have never before known," she says. "I knew that God was calling me to live a consecrated life. When you know something like that, you must act on it."

"I knew nothing about religious life, but I knew that God could do anything. I woke up in the middle of the academic year and knew I needed to enter a religious community. The first three communities I wrote to did not respond. I was in New York and had heard of Cardinal O'Connor's efforts to start a religious community, so I thought I ought to at least look into it. That summer I joined."

Up until his life's end, Cardinal O'Connor held a special place for the order he founded. He frequently visited the convent and invited the sisters to dine with him. That affinity extended even after his death on May 3, 2000. Cardinal O'Connor asked that front pews in the Church be reserved for the sisters, and he also provided for the order in his will.

"He was our spiritual father and our founder," says Mother Agnes. "He led us to understand our particular charism in the Eucharist and reverence for human life. We see ourselves as women of the Eucharist and women of the Church. We are spiritual daughters of John Cardinal O'Connor who was such a wonderful voice for the sacredness of human life."

Young and Catholic

The Bronx Friars

The gray-habited young men with shorn heads and long beards can be seen on the streets of Harlem. They live and work among the poor, teaching, praying, and occasionally skateboarding. They belong to the Franciscan Friars of Renewal, an order that has experienced phenomenal growth since its founding. Started sixteen years ago with just eight men, the Franciscan Friars of the Renewal have now grown to a hundred men, and a separate order of twelve sisters. Twenty-five men entered in the fall of 2003 alone. The friars operate three friaries in the Bronx, two in Yonkers, one in Harlem, one in England, and another in Honduras. Identifiable by their gray habits, most of them aren't gray anywhere else; the friars have a mean age of about thirty-two.

"When I pass on, it will be about twenty-nine," jokes Fr. Benedict Groeschel, the order's well-known co-founder, author, and speaker. He says the younger numbers do not surprise him. He describes the attraction to orders such as the friars as a reaction to "liminality" — the wider culture's efforts to "push the limits."

"Young people are tired of everything being up for grabs. They don't want to join the Sisters of Inimitable Confusion. They are yearning for structure," he adds.

"We stick out in a crowd," comments Fr. Glen Sudano, superior of the community. "The young are attracted by our strong identity and purpose."

Fr. Joseph Mary, thirty-four, originally from Laurel, Maryland, agrees. He says he was attracted to the Franciscan Friars by their "joyfulness, fraternity, spirituality, and devotion to the Holy Father and the Magisterium."

"Many of the men who come to us have had conversions in college," says Fr. Sudano. "Many have not led lives that would seem typical of religious life, but they tired of hanging from the chandeliers.

"The charismatic renewal, eucharistic adoration, and Marian devotion are strong elements for those coming in," Fr. Sudano adds. "They have a clear recognition that Pope John Paul II is a prophet for our times, and they are seeking not just community, but a viable family life."

One of the secrets to the friars' success is stability, stemming from the family backgrounds of those entering the community.

"When I sit down with a guy," says Fr. Sudano, "I ask him in the middle of my interview, 'Did you have a happy childhood?' The biggest factor for success are those families where the mother and the father have stayed together and there are no traumatic events in early childhood — no abuse or divorce, no emotional or moral trauma, no strong addictions. We look for a healthy, balanced person. There you can plant the seeds because the soil is not poisoned."

The friars are also attracting religious vocations from overseas.

"It appears that Europeans are making the leap across the pond to find religious life," says Fr. Sudano. The community has a few men from England, one from Ireland, two from Poland, one from Lebanon, five from France, and one from former East Germany.

The community's vocation director is Fr. Luke Mary Fletcher, thirty-one, from Tipton, Indiana. Like many in the community, Fr. Fletcher had a religious conversion during college.

"Partly through a religious pilgrimage, I saw the darkness that I had been in, chasing after all of the things that the world tells us will make us happy," he recalls. "As I encountered Christ, especially in the Eucharist, I started to realize the darkness that my peers and I were in. I wanted to serve God, but I didn't know how."

At that, Fletcher began visiting various religious orders.

"I found myself very discouraged by what I found," he describes. "Some would greet me, not wearing any clerics, and tell me that I was their first vocation in twenty-five years." Eventually, through the Franciscans at Marytown, Fletcher discovered that he had a strong attraction to the example of St. Francis.

After going through the Pre-Theologate program at Steubenville, Fletcher still wasn't certain where he belonged.

"People joke that not even God knows how many different Franciscan orders there are," says Father Fletcher. "Many people kept telling me that I should look into *those* friars in New York, but being from a small town, I had no interest at all."

He was about ready to join an order, despite his list of gripes, when he discovered the Franciscan Friars of Renewal at vocation day on campus. "Here was an order that had unwavering fidelity to the Holy Father, eucharistic adoration, authenticity in being poor and working with the poor, devotion to the Holy Mother, and was pro-life," he explains. "I hadn't found all of that anywhere until I ran into the friars."

Twenty-four hours after visiting the order, Fletcher knew it was where he wanted to spend the rest of his life. He says that his time with the friars has been all that he hoped it would be, and more.

"What I found here was so different," explains Fr. Fletcher. "I've found manly Christ-centered relationships. There is also a joy — a certain sense of the Holy Spirit — that is hard to put your finger on."

As an example, Fr. Fletcher explains the unconventional evangelization practices of fellow friar, Br. Pio Mary. A talented skateboarder, Br. Pio engages in skateboard evangelization — skating around the Bronx, handing out Miraculous Medals to crowds of youth. Fr. Fletcher recalls when Br. Pio came to his hometown of Tipton, Indiana.

A New Generation Answers the Vocational Call

"In one day, he met all of the young people in my hometown," laughs Fr. Fletcher.

The order continues to receive between twelve and fifteen vocations each year. Fr. Fletcher says that the young men learn about the friars in a variety of ways — through retreats, word of mouth, their website, and personal encounters. Many priests, says Fr. Fletcher, keep lists of where they can send young people.

"It's like a snowball," he adds. "Once it gets some momentum, it keeps going."

That momentum is also occurring at some Franciscan women's orders.

∞

Ohio's Sisters of the Sorrowful Mother

Gray habits and white veils can often be seen on the campus at Franciscan University of Steubenville. The Franciscan Third Order Regular, Sisters of the Sorrowful Mother is located just a few miles north of Steubenville in Toronto, Ohio. While not as large as some of the other orders, it continues to attract young women and has steadily been growing since its founding.

The community was officially established on August 15, 1988, the Feast of the Assumption, in the Diocese of Steubenville by then-Bishop Albert Ottenweller.

While the sisters are active in numerous ministries — prison ministry, parish missions, hospital and shut-in visits, vacation Bible school, and Confirmation retreats, their work flows from their prayer life. A contemplative-active order, the sisters spend four to six hours per day in prayer, including daily Mass, the Rosary, and eucharistic adoration. The order's mission house in Steubenville is situated among the materially poor. A second mission home has been established in Gaming, Austria. Their motherhouse and the order's hermitages are set in a more contemplative setting in the country on a hill in Toronto, Ohio.

The average age of the twenty-seven sisters living within the community is thirty-four.

"There is something definitely going on," says St. Catherine Lynn Forsythe, vocations director for the Franciscan Sisters. "The young are just clamoring to learn about vocations. We've seen an increased interest, especially over the past four years."

Sr. Forsythe says that when they used to attend youth conferences, the young people used to avoid speaking with the sisters, but there is now a growing openness among them.

"We're often invited to attend Youth 2000 retreats, and we're one of the few orders that visit elementary and high schools in our area," she explains. "Sixty girls, ages six to thirteen, attended our day of vocation awareness."

A child of Anglican converts to the Faith, Sr. Forsythe says that her parents were well-catechized.

"Throughout my twenties, I was still dating and open to whatever," says Sr. Forsythe. "I didn't have a deep desire for religious life."

All through college, she felt increasingly that God was calling her to something more. Every day, after teaching at a Montesorri school, she would spend an hour in prayer in eucharistic adoration. "I would pray Psalm 37:4 — 'If you delight in the Lord, He will give you the desire of your heart.' I knew that God would make His heart mine and make His desire my own."

Two years later, after attending a dance with friends and meeting a man, she started thinking about marriage again. Not long afterward, while in adoration, she heard in her mind, "You belong to me, and you will never belong to another."

"I had never heard anything so clear," she recalls.

A New Generation Answers the Vocational Call

While on a retreat at a Cistercian monastery, Forsythe chanted the office for the first time.

"I didn't know what that was, but I knew I had to have it," she says. That week, she began reading the Vatican documents on religious life. "It was like reading my journal. These vows were what I was made for."

At the age of thirty, she entered the Companions of the Cross, a new society of apostolic life in Ottawa, Ontario, and was preparing to become a sister. In the end, she came to the Sisters of the Sorrowful Mother because she was attracted to the contemplative life.

"I was attracted by the silence and the solitude and the Franciscan peace," she says.

Women, she says, are drawn to the order for a variety of reasons. They learn of the order from their presence at youth conferences. They find the sisters on the Internet. The order's habits are a witness to others.

"The habit and the veil set you apart," says Sr. Forsythe. "It reminds me every morning, when I put it on, of who I belong to." She adds that it also reflects the Holy Father's new feminism. "The dress is appropriate to the dignity of a sister as a bride and mother. College women can reflect on that before they reflect on their religious vocation."

∞

Ann Arbor's Sisters of Mary, Mother of the Eucharist
Established only six years ago, Ann Arbor's Dominican Sisters of Mary, Mother of the Eucharist is another example of an order that has witnessed extraordinary success in a short time.

At a time when the average American sister is in her sixties, the majority of the Sisters of Mary are in their twenties. Since their founding in 1997, the community has grown tenfold from four sisters to forty-five. A teaching order, the Sisters of Mary operate four schools known as the Spiritus Sanctus Academies in Ann Arbor, Michigan.

The order was founded by Sr. Joseph Andrew Bogdanowicz, Sr. John Dominic Rasmussen, Sr. Mary Samuel Handwerker, and Mother Mary Assumpta, former prioress general of the Dominican Sisters of St. Cecilia in Nashville. During the early 1990s, Mother Assumpta helped New York's John Cardinal O'Connor form the Sisters of Life.

"Our community is a community for the new evangelization," says Sr. Joseph Andrew Bogdanowicz, vocations director for the order.

Like the other orders that are thriving, the Sisters of Mary wear a habit.

"A habit makes a definite statement of a radical life in God, that she is set apart to belong totally to Christ for others," explains Sr. Joseph. "Young people today are very capable of heroic sacrifices. They love challenges."

She says that the community is growing because "we are what the Church calls us to be. Our center is the Eucharist, and we strive to be Mary in the Church today. The joy is obvious."

Some of the community's recent vocations include a lawyer who was making a six-figure income in New York City, a missionary who had worked in Belize, a college graduate who had worked with displaced persons in Moscow, and a seventeen-year-old who had lived in Spain. "There is no typical vocation," says Sr. Joseph.

Wherever she travels, she says, the young are attracted to their way of life.

"We were invited to staff a booth with [apologetics apostolate] Catholic Answers at an art fair at the University of Michigan," says Sr. Joseph. "On the way there, I felt someone tugging on my cape. When I turned around, there was this young person who asked, 'Who are you and where did you come from and tell me all about it. If we live the authentic religious life, the vocations are numerous."

They receive religious vocations with absolutely no advertising. "We never advertise," says Sr. Joseph. "If I had money like that, I would make a bunch more holy cards and drop them. It is the Eucharist who is sending them. God is doing it."

∞

Finding Vocations in the Most Unlikely Places

Religious vocations sometimes come from the most unlikely places. The Newman Foundation at the University of Illinois, Champaign-Urbana has witnessed dramatic success. The Foundation includes a Newman library, residence halls for men and women, a dining hall, computer lab, four religion courses that students may take for university credit, and St. John's Catholic Chapel. The chapel seats eight hundred and provides six Masses each Sunday, plus three each weekday.

"Here, it's like the ghetto of Catholicism," says Fr. Brian Herlocker, "so everyone is fervent about their faith." Approximately twelve thousand of the campus's thirty-five thousand students are Catholic.

Herlocker estimates that they have ten to fifteen students each year go on to pursue a religious vocation.

"Catholics live in the dorm and interact. Other students who come here end up being affected by that," he adds.

Lutheran convert Dr. Kenneth Howell and Msgr. Stuart Swetland head up the foundation and teach four classes on campus — U.S. Catholic Experience, the Basics of Catholicism, Catholic

Young and Catholic

Social Tradition, and Topics in Catholicism. In union with the FOCUS missionaries on campus, Herlocker estimates that between five and six hundred students are involved in Bible studies or catechesis in some way. The Samuel Group is a group of students who meet for about five hours once a month for formal vocation discernment.

Texas A&M's St. Mary's Student Center has witnessed similar results. Fr. Todd Reitmeyer, a priest for the Diocese of Sioux Falls, South Dakota, speaks highly of the young-adult program offered through his alma mater.

"The student center has had great success in fostering vocations," Reitmeyer says. "There are presently more than forty former Texas A&M students pursuing vocations in various dioceses and religious orders."

In addition to reaching more than ten thousand students through Holy Mass each week, the center also hosts a variety of retreats and events to educate young adults about their Faith.

Two popular outreach programs are the student center's Nun Run and Seminary Sprint. Developed in 1995, the events gather separate groups of young men and women who are discerning a vocation, and during spring break, they each take trips to visit a number of monasteries or convents.

"This allows them to discern different charisms and see what [religious] life is like," Reitmeyer explains.

"We have visited religious orders as far away as Nashville, Kentucky, and St. Louis," says Martha Tonn, RCIA director at the center. "Students get an opportunity to see active and contemplative orders as well as those with apostolates such as health care or education."

Judging from the statistics, the center's efforts are a success. In the last six years alone, the center has had fifty participants enter seminaries, convents, or monasteries, with forty-eight currently in active formation.

Religious vocations still come, as they often have, from larger families. There has also been recognition by many diocesan vocation directors that homeschooling is where many future ecclesial vocations will come.

"Homeschooling families love children and are open to having children. We are already starting to see vocations from home-schooling families," says Fr. Gregory Mastey, vocations director for the Diocese of St. Cloud, Minnesota. Mastey says he is aware of a handful of young men from homeschooled families who have recently entered seminary.

The Archdiocese of St. Paul-Minneapolis ordained its first homeschooled priest, Fr. Daniel Haugen, in 2003.

"Large families breed a generous spirit," says Benedictine Fr. Paul Marx, former director of Human Life International. Fr. Marx is one of four religious vocations in his own family of fourteen children. "That generosity leads to religious vocations."

Obviously, not all the news is doom and gloom, as some would have us believe. While some geographic areas are experiencing priest shortages, a great many other areas are not. Whether single, married, or religious vocations, the Holy Spirit is active in the Church. Young men and women are answering Christ's call.

∞

Holiness Is Always Youthful

Saints for the Future

*"I love saying a prayer to the Lord written by
St. Thomas Aquinas or St. Teresa of Avila.
It's wonderful to think that they may be
saying these very prayers along with me in heaven."*

Jared Black, 21, college student, Bremerton, Washington

∞

Stella Marie Jeffrey, director for evangelization and catechesis with the Diocese of Fargo, recalled a conversation she had at a national conference with a group of diocesan directors.

"The directors were discussing a survey that they were conducting when they said that the greatest threat to the Church was the increase of conservative, pre-Vatican II thinking," said Jeffrey.

When Jeffrey suggested that such terms were hard to understand and asked for a definition, someone shot back, "You know. They think pre-Vatican II."

"My parents weren't even married yet back then," responded Jeffrey.

"We all know it means those who embrace the institutional Church," another colleague offered.

When Jeffrey shared that she felt that the institutional Church was of divine origin, no one knew how to respond. "The conversation ended with one director saying that we can't force our religion on people," said Jeffrey. "A friend asked, 'Then why did Jesus die?' The response was, 'Jesus isn't *the* way; He is *a* way.'"

Today's young Catholics have not taken up the causes of the older generation. Vatican II is not their fight. Most hadn't even been born when the council took place. The fight of the middle-aged — the conflict between liberal dissent and conservative orthodoxy — has no appeal for the young. They embrace the Church and its teachings, sometimes regardless of the faith of their parents. This is evident in the way that the younger generation thinks, acts, and prays.

"The young today are living the tragedy of the choices we made, and many of them want no part of it," says Anne Marie Cosgrove, director of Silent No More Minnesota, an outreach program for post-abortive men and women. "They look at us and think our generation has really messed up."

Jeffrey agrees. "Their generation gave us prominent divorce, legal abortion, and euthanasia. Why would we want to be like them?"

In an address for the Pontifical Council for the Laity's eighth International Youth Forum in 2004, Harvard law professor Mary Ann Glendon described the "millennial generation" as one that is searching. They are "a generation of young men and women who want something better for themselves and their future children than what has been handed on to them; a generation that is exploring uncharted territory and finding little guidance from its elders," she said.

In many ways, the young faithful look nothing like the generation that has gone before. Unlike the previous generation, which longed for experimentation, Generations X and Y long for authenticity. Rather than saying one thing and doing another, they long for a Faith that is consistent with their practice — what some observers have termed "orthopraxis."

The prolific British author and convert G. K. Chesterton once said, "Saints are those who exaggerate what the world has forgotten." This can be seen quite clearly in the way young Catholics live.

Faithful young-adult Catholics are embracing countercultural practices such as abstinence before marriage and Natural Family

Planning. They overwhelmingly reject legalized abortion. They are eager to learn about the Pope's vision of the dignity of the person, and they are increasingly drawn to incorporate devotional practices into their daily lives. Whether they realize it or not, they are responding to the Second Vatican Council's call to universal holiness. They are potential saints for the future.

Even in the secular culture, there is mounting evidence to suggest that the young are rejecting the message of sexual liberation touted by the media and the previous generation. More than a million teens and college students are registered with True Love Waits, one of many national abstinence campaigns. A National Institutes of Health study released in 2003 demonstrates the importance of religion. It notes that girls, in particular, with strong religious views were less likely to engage in sexual activity than less religious teens.[23]

According to a 2003 survey of teenagers and young adults conducted for the National Campaign to Prevent Teen Pregnancy, eighty-five percent of teens believe that sex should occur only in long-term committed relationships. Two-thirds of U.S. teenagers who admit having sexual relations say they wished that they had waited longer.

"The youth are really starting to question the messages of the world regarding premarital relationships and abortion," says thirty-four-year-old former model Constance Coxon, who works with the young to promote Catholic Christian values and is finishing her degree in religious studies at Rome's Pontifical University Regina Apostolorum. Her thesis is on how to rescue young women

[23] "Abstinence, the New Wave in Sex Education," *Zenit*, July 5, 2003.

from modern-day secularism. "There are seeds being planted all over the place," she added. "Christ is preparing His Church for a new generation."

∽

Worth Waiting For

Two years ago, as a high school junior, Jason Buck founded the first pro-life club at his all-male Catholic school, Malvern Preparatory School in Malvern, Pennsylvania.

"The men needed something they could stand up for, and chastity and the unborn were perfect," says Buck.

One Wednesday evening per month Malvern Prep Men for Life would conduct a prayerful protest at the local abortion site, inviting nearby public- and Catholic-school peers.

Some of the school's teachers and the student newspaper questioned the message of the group.

"Pro-abortion-minded students resented us and made it their mission to criticize us," Buck says. "Yet we stuck it out and have made an impact not only in Philadelphia but across the country."

On Valentine's Day 2001, the Men for Life began their chastity project. They ordered two hundred white roses and placed them in vases on the lunch tables at their sister all-girl school, Villa Maria Academy. The roses were accompanied by stickers giving ten reasons to save sex for marriage. Cards read: "We at Malvern Prep Men for Life think you're special, and you're worth waiting for."

Some female students wore their stickers all week, and they talked about the roses for months afterward.

"Trying to meet guys who share similar values is difficult," says 2002 Villa Maria graduate Christina Vetre. "We took the gesture very seriously."

An article in the *National Catholic Register* led other schools nationwide to start their own pro-life groups, and many replicated the gift of the roses as a way of spreading the message of chastity.

Popular chastity speaker Jason Evert, of San Diego–based Catholic Answers, also adopted the gesture. After his presentations at high schools, young men deliver roses to the young women in the audience.

Now a freshman at Franciscan University of Steubenville, Buck continues to speak to high school students and has authored a manual on how to start a pro-life youth group.

Of the more than one hundred member organizations of the Sioux Falls, South Dakota-based National Abstinence Clearinghouse, one that has arisen specifically to address abstinence is Project Reality. The Illinois-based organization has identified and supported more than thirty Miss America candidates who have chosen abstinence as their platform. Among them are 2003 Miss America Erika Harold, and former Miss Wisconsin, Mary-Louise Kurey.

∞

Standing with Courage

At age fifteen, Mary-Louise Kurey missed an opportunity to witness to a friend. She has been making up for it ever since.

Born in upstate New York, Kurey and her family moved to Wisconsin when she was seven years old. The youngest of four children, she says that she grew up in a fairly strict home. "My older siblings say that I had more freedom than they did," she says. "Neither my brothers, nor my sister, were allowed to date in high school, but I was."

Kurey attended Catholic schools through fifth grade, and then attended a public school. It was there that she missed her first opportunity to use her voice — a mistake she vowed she would not make again.

"In seventh grade, many of my classmates were becoming sexually active and using drugs," recalls Kurey. "The student who had a locker right next to mine used cocaine." Because of Kurey's upbringing, she naturally resisted such practices. As a consequence, Kurey decided she would not use drugs or alcohol. She also decided that she would be chaste until marriage.

"At that time, I felt that what my friends were doing wasn't any of my business," says Kurey. "One of my friends became pregnant at fifteen. That was a real wake-up call for me because I wondered what might have happened if I had done the right thing and witnessed to her."

In college, another close friend had a nervous breakdown. "When I visited her in the hospital, I learned that it was the result of an abortion she had had three years earlier. All the while, I felt I had been taking good care of myself, while allowing my friends to make destructive choices. Those events made me realize that I had a calling to speak out so that others would not have to suffer the way my friends had suffered in their lives." Ever since, that's just what Kurey has done.

Kurey got her start in pageants when she was crowned Milwaukee's Junior Miss. Following high school, she competed in Milwaukee's Miss Polish Festival, and in a strange reversal of Pope John Paul II's election as the first Polish pope in Italy, Kurey became Milwaukee's first Miss Polish Fest of Italian descent. She later ranked in the top ten at the Miss Wisconsin pageant. "At that point, I said that I was never doing pageant work again," says Kurey.

Kurey received her undergraduate degree in voice performance from the University of Eau Claire, followed by a degree in opera at

Duquesne University. While at Duquesne, Kurey began speaking to students about chastity. "I realized that if I had a title, I would be able to reach more people with my message," says Kurey. So, at the age of twenty-two, she returned to pageant work, eventually being named Miss Wisconsin during her final eligible year, 1999.

After winning Miss Wisconsin, Kurey was told that some states did not want women speaking on an abstinence platform. According to Kurey, the Miss America pageant contacted the Wisconsin state board to ask if she would change her platform. "They told me that I could change my platform to character education and have abstinence be a part of it," says Kurey.

In the end, Kurey decided not to. She ended up taking the top honors in Talent and was among the ten finalists in that year's Miss America pageant. "A lot of people told me that if I had changed my platform, I would have done better," says Kurey, "but I have no regrets. God has blessed my work."

With a crown and title in hand, Kurey then used her reign as Miss Wisconsin to travel the world speaking to more than a hundred thousand teens about chastity. She describes her interaction with students as the most rewarding part of her time as Miss Wisconsin.

"Many would come up to me afterward and share their stories," Kurey says. "They would tell me that they had had sex and that they regretted it. They seemed relieved to hear that they could start over and make a new beginning. Young men would come up to say that they were virgins and that in the past they were ashamed to admit it. Now, they realized that their virginity was an awesome gift to give to their future spouse, and they feel proud. It's wonderful to know that you are making that kind of impact."

She recalls the reaction from one young man after speaking to a church group. "He came up and asked me to write 'Virgin' in big letters on the back of his T-shirt," says Kurey. "He was a senior and the captain of the football team. I asked him if he was sure he wanted me to do that, and he said, 'Sure, I'm proud of it.' I asked him if I could write something else, and so I wrote 'Virgin and Studly.' Many of the girls started laughing and screaming. Two years later, when I was speaking in the same area, some students told me that he still wears the shirt."

Not only did Kurey speak to teens during her reign, but she also appeared on several television shows, including *Inside Edition*, *Sally Jessy Raphael*, and five appearances on Bill Maher's *Politically Incorrect*.

On one of those shows, she even won the respect of a *Playboy* playmate.

"She told me that she couldn't do what I was doing, but she admired me for doing it. She said, 'Good luck with your mission,' " explains Kurey.

In April 2002, Kurey also testified before Congress on abstinence education. Her experiences led her to publish a book — *Standing with Courage: Confronting Tough Decisions about Sex*. The book, written for teens and young adults, addresses issues pertaining to young people's lives — peer pressure, sex and relationships, drug use, self-image, and standing up for what you believe in.

"According to the National Campaign to Prevent Teen Pregnancy," says Kurey, "ninety-three percent of teens feel that they should be given the message that abstinence is the best choice, and the majority of teens who have been sexually active regret it. Parents believe that they have little control over their teens' behavior. They feel that teens are going to engage in sex anyway, but this is not true. A recent CDC study showed that fifty-four percent of high school students are virgins. Another study showed that teen girls who are close to their mothers are much less likely to be sexually active. All the teens I have talked to want to be close to their parents. Parents, therefore, have a huge impact over their teen's choices by communicating to them that they believe they can wait and that they believe that waiting is the best choice."

Married in 2004, Kurey now serves as director of the pro-life office for the Archdiocese of Chicago.

"Looking back," she says, "I can now say that the choice I made in seventh grade was the best choice I have ever made."

∞

Embracing Natural Family Planning

In addition to the young embracing the message of abstinence, young married couples are increasingly supporting the Church's teaching against contraception by learning modern, scientific methods of Natural Family Planning.

"The numbers usually given are that between five and seven percent of Catholics use Natural Family Planning," says Sue Ek, director of the Billings Ovulation Method, USA, "but those numbers are growing."

The demand for Natural Family Planning services in places such as Atlanta and New York has increased. Whereas there used to be two NFP teaching couples in the Atlanta Archdiocese in 1991, today there are twenty-one certified teachers, teaching in three languages.

NFP-only OB-GYN, Dr. Kathleen Raviele explains how a Familia, a small-group study circle for young mothers, contributed to a greater understanding and acceptance of NFP among the women involved.

"Despite initial opposition to the teaching," writes Raviele, "after a priest explained the Church's teachings on marriage, sexual intercourse within marriage, and the role of children, the women understood and accepted the Church's teaching." Furthermore, explains Raviele, one woman went on to become an NFP teacher, and another started implanting the eight embryos she had in frozen storage from the *in vitro* fertilization that she had not previously realized was wrong.[24]

Even more so, Ek and Raviele note that the numbers of physicians who are converting their practices to NFP-only are increasing. As their numbers rise, so, too, will the numbers of those using the practice.

It used to be that "NFP-only" physicians — doctors who don't prescribe contraceptives, and who understand and promote modern, scientific methods of Natural Family Planning — were difficult to find. That's less so today. Not only are there more NFP-only physicians than there were six years ago, but more and more are coming to the decision earlier in their careers.

Approximately six years ago, Steve Koob, director of the apostolate One More Soul, based in Dayton, Ohio, created the country's first directory of NFP-only physicians. It began with forty-five doctors from a variety of specialties and has now grown to contain more than 450. "We get about three new NFP-only physicians each month," says Koob.

Many of the physicians profiled in One More Soul's directory came to be NFP-only at the admonition of clergy. That is certainly true for Dr. Michael Skoch of Lincoln, Nebraska.

"I had been trained at a Catholic hospital in Wichita, Kansas, and [contraception] was what we were taught, so I assumed that it must be okay for me to prescribe," says Skoch.

[24] Kathleen Raviele, "Living With Your Fertility: A Presentation for All Dioceses and All Methods," USCCB Forum, Winter/Spring 2004, Vol. 15, Nos. 1 and 2.

Eighteen months into his practice, Skoch found his professional life being questioned by his local priest. "He asked me if I knew what I was doing," says Skoch. "When I told him I was doing what I had been taught, he replied that if I continued doing what I was doing, he could not continue giving me Holy Communion." A year and a half later, Skoch finally stopped prescribing contraception.

In June 2000, Skoch left his family practice to launch the Moscati Health Center — a four-physician primary-care medical practice incorporated with mental-health services that does not compromise Skoch's values.

While Skoch says that he did lose some patients during the transition, he estimates that ninety percent of his two thousand families stayed with him.

For Skoch, the decision to become NFP-only came mid-career. However, an increasing number of physicians are embracing NFP during residency or before. It's a trend that Skoch has noticed.

"More and more young men and women have this figured out at a much earlier stage than I did," says Skoch. "It's an inspiration to me at this stage of my life. I firmly believe that the future is really bright and positive in this direction."

Dr. Richard Cash is among those who've made that choice. Cash decided to go NFP-only during his third and fourth years of medical school, when he became aware of information that he hadn't been taught, or had ignored, about the abortifacient potential of oral contraceptives.

Cash was awarded the Minnesota Academy of Family Practice Resident of the Year award in 2002 and is in his second year of family practice with the St. Cloud Medical Group. He serves as one of two NFP-only physicians in the forty-five-member practice.

"When I made the decision to focus on NFP, I knew that the pill was used to treat the symptoms of a lot of different conditions," says Cash. "I wanted the knowledge to be able to offer something more for my patients rather than saying, 'I'm sorry, I don't deal with that.'"

So, in 2003, Cash was certified as an NFP medical consultant by completing a six-month program through the Omaha-based Pope Paul VI Institute.

"That training will help me better treat some gynecologic conditions without using artificial hormones," he says. "It's a disease-based approach," he explains, "meaning that a lot of things that women have, such as infertility, painful menses, and ovarian cysts are symptoms of an underlying disease that is not often sought after by the medical community. They simply cover it up with contraceptives."

Cash says that he has seen a trend among younger physicians embracing the Church's teaching. "The majority of people in the medical consultant program were students, residents, or physicians early in their practice," notes Cash.

Another physician who came to the decision early on is fourth-year Ohio State University medical student Kyle Beiter. A biology major from Franciscan University of Steubenville, Beiter hopes to bring an NFP-approach to his work as an OB-GYN resident at Georgetown.

Beiter has found the support that he needs along the way. He says he was fortunate to do his rotations with mentor Dr. Michael Parker, an NFP-only physician at Grant Hospital in Columbus. In addition, in preparation for his residency work, Beiter spoke with colleague Dr. Faith Daggs, a Camp Hill, Pennsylvania OB-GYN.

"She went to Georgetown," says Beiter, "and was kind of anxious going into it. Yet her peers supported her decision. She has been out for five years and is doing well."

Clearly, the role of doctors is pivotal.

"The doctors are huge on this issue," says Theresa Notare, assistant director of the U.S. Catholic Bishops' Diocesan Development Program for Natural Family Planning. "Outside of the priest, if a couple is having trouble on this front, they will go to their doctor, and they will take what he says very seriously."

As important as the doctors are, the support of NFP teaching couples and of the Church is just as crucial. Notare describes it as a "trinity of support."

"Whenever we survey the dioceses about the obstacles that stand in their way of getting the Church's NFP message out to people, they include priests not speaking about birth control and NFP, couples not coming forward to witness or teach other couples, and then, of course, the medical profession," says Notare.

NFP apostolates have undertaken a number of efforts to support bishops and priests in encouraging them to speak about birth control and Natural Family Planning. The Diocese of St. Cloud's Natural Family Planning office released an audiotape and book titled *A Preachable Message: The Dynamics of Preaching Natural Family Planning*, featuring sample homilies from Chicago's Cardinal Francis George, Denver's Archbishop Charles Chaput, and Phoenix's Bishop Thomas Olmsted.

Recognizing that the message is not often preached from the pulpit, Fr. Daniel McCaffrey has established NFP Outreach, an apostolate in the Oklahoma City Archdiocese, as a way of spreading

Theresa Notare, assistant director of the U.S. Catholic Bishops' Diocesan Development Program for Natural Family Planning, is encouraged by the increased interest in NFP and believes that doctors have an important role to play in promoting it.

the "good news" of NFP. He travels the country, delivering the NFP homilies that pastors are often reticent to deliver.

Notare is hopeful. "I'm very encouraged when I see the young people who have somehow stumbled onto Natural Family Planning and the Theology of the Body," says Notare. "They are just jazzed about this. There is great hope out there."

New York's Peter McFadden, founder of the *Love and Responsibility* discussion group, agrees. "NFP has a logic of its own," says McFadden. "Prior to teaching it through our Pre-Cana program, there were fewer than five couples practicing the Creighton model of NFP in New York City. At our first Pre-Cana program, we signed up three couples to learn it, so we've already doubled the number of people using it. It's just going to continue to build and build."

Notare's observation seems to be on the mark. The proliferation of Theology of the Body discussion groups and an explosion of new books and materials on the topic are leading more and more young people to embrace the beauty of the Church's teaching regarding human sexuality. The reality of the Holy Father's teachings can be witnessed through their impact on how Catholic couples live out their married relationship.

Thirty-seven-year-old Stacey Johnson of Hinesville, Georgia, is convinced that acceptance of the Church's teaching on human sexuality saved her marriage, if not from certain divorce, at least from becoming an empty imitation of God's plan for married love.

Stacey and her husband, Michael, first met as students at West Point. Married in 1988, they used contraception for the first nine years of their marriage.

After the birth of their second child, they spoke of Michael's getting a vasectomy.

Stacey explains that they made the decision for what they thought were all the right reasons. Stacey's pregnancies had been difficult, and with Michael in the Army, he was often gone for long periods.

"We were serious about being sterile," says Stacey, "and our families supported us in that decision."

In 1994, Michael had the vasectomy. Immediately afterward, Stacey says that she experienced a great sense of loss.

"Something felt wrong," says Stacey. "I remember feeling empty and wishing that the surgery hadn't worked."

Both had thought the operation would improve their sexual relationship. It didn't.

"We were just going through the motions," explains Stacey.

"Michael worked long hours. We didn't talk much. We were two people who lived in the same house. We were just using each other for gratification," says Stacey.

"We hadn't only lost sight of what marriage was supposed to be," says Stacey. "We didn't know, as Catholics or as a married couple, what was the purpose for marriage and sexuality."

Their oldest son suffered from a form of autism, and in 1997, Stacey decided to homeschool their children. That's when everything changed. "I decided that if I was going to teach my children what we believe as Catholics, I thought I should probably know more about it myself," says Stacey.

At about the same time, Stacey decided to sponsor a candidate in her parish's RCIA program. One of the books they were required to read was *Rome Sweet Home*, by Catholic converts Scott and Kimberly Hahn.

"Scott Hahn's explanation of what the Church teaches on contraception and sterilization was beautiful. It made so much sense," she recalls.

When Stacey showed the book to her husband, he wholeheartedly agreed.

"We felt as if we had stolen from God, and that we needed Michael to undergo a reversal to make everything right," says Stacey.

In 1997, Michael had a reversal of his vasectomy.

"Apart from getting married," says Michael, "having the reversal was the best decision I've ever made."

They conceived soon after. Their third child, Jacob, was born prematurely at thirty weeks and spent seven weeks in the hospital.

Frightened about the possibility of becoming pregnant immediately after the birth of Jacob, Stacey went through the Couple to Couple League's home-study course to learn the sympto-thermal method of NFP.

Not only did practicing NFP force Stacey and Michael to communicate more, but it also helped them to see God's purpose for their marriage, and improved their relationship.

"That has made all the difference in the world," she says, "It helped us to appreciate each other as a gift from God, and helped us not to take our children for granted."

Since that time, the Johnsons have given birth to their fourth child, Madeleine, and are hoping for more. A lieutenant colonel, Michael spent January through August 2003 in Iraq, and has been repeatedly deployed for long periods.

"While it's still hard to be apart, we find that practicing NFP led to increased communication and a greater appreciation for our marriage and God's plan for it," says Stacy. "We're growing closer together and closer to God, which makes the readjustment easier when Michael comes home. It's like he's been gone for the weekend."

Not only are young Catholics discovering the truths in the Church's teachings about fertility, but it also appears that they are far more open to having children.

Demographer Phillip Longman, a senior fellow at the New America Foundation, has noted the steep demographic decline taking place around the world. Japanese fertility rates have been below replacement levels since the mid-1950s, and the last time Europeans produced enough children to reproduce themselves was the mid-1970s.

In the journal *Foreign Affairs,* he asks the question, "Where will the children of the future come from?" His answer: they will come "from people who are at odds with the modern environment," notably those people with strong religious convictions.

"Does this mean that the future belongs to those who believe they are — or who are in fact — commanded by a higher power to procreate?" wonders Longman. "Based on current trends, the answer appears to be yes."

Longman's statistics demonstrate a strong correlation between religious conviction and high fertility. In the United States, for example, forty percent of people who attend church weekly say that the ideal family size is three or more, as compared with only twenty-seven percent of those who seldom attend church.[25]

His findings indicate that the Church of the future belongs, in part, to those who bear children. The repercussions of such a demographic shift are natural. Those who believe that children are a gift from God will have more children. Those who feel otherwise will not. Consequently, Churchgoers would expect to see their numbers increase over time.

This argument has also been used to explain the demographic shift taking place on the issue of abortion.

The *Wall Street Journal*'s James Taranto has suggested that abortion depletes the next generation of pro-abortion voters more than pro-life voters, eventually creating a more pro-life population. He

---

[25] Phillip Longman, "The Global Baby Bust," *Foreign Affairs,* May/June 2004.

terms the phenomenon as the "Roe effect."[26] Again, those who are pro-life would naturally be expected to have more children than those who are not. That would lead to an increase in numbers of those who are pro-life.

∞

The Turn of the Tide on Abortion

Recent surveys suggest that the tide is turning on the abortion issue as increasing numbers of young people oppose abortion.[27] A November 2003 Gallup youth survey found that seventy-two percent of teenagers found abortion morally unacceptable. A 2004 Zogby poll found similar results.

Statistics demonstrate that the young are less likely than their parents to support abortion-on-demand. That observation is most clearly demonstrated by the increasingly large numbers of young people present at the March for Life held in Washington, D.C., each January 22.

"For every adult over thirty, there were ten young people under thirty," says Ann Marie Cosgrove, director of Silent No More Minnesota, of the 2004 March for Life. "These kids get it that a huge part of their generation is missing, and they want something done about it. They are the voice we will be hearing."

Polls in recent years demonstrate that teenagers and college-age Americans are more pro-life than their counterparts were a generation ago. According to the *New York Times*, a study of

[26] James Taranto, "Quantifying the Roe Effect," *Wall Street Journal*, March 5, 2004.

[27] *The American Freshman: National Norms for Fall 1998*, Los Angeles: Higher Education Research Institute, U.C.L.A., Graduate School of Education and Information Studies, 2003.

American college freshmen shows that support for abortion has been dropping since the early Nineties. A New York Times/CBS News poll conducted in January 2003 found that among people ages eighteen to twenty-nine, only thirty-nine percent agreed that abortion should be available to those who want it. That percentage is down from nearly half the respondents as recently as 1993.[28]

Experts cite a variety of reasons for the increased support for the pro-life position. Among them are the availability of ultrasound technology, the tendency for pro-life supporters to have larger families, and an increased receptiveness to the pro-life message.

In 2003, Gudrun Lang, director of the European branch of the World Youth Alliance, spoke before the European Parliament. There, she described her peers:

> It is my generation that is the first to experience what it means to live in a more or less "value-less" continent. It is we who witness a society of broken families — you are aware of what that entails for the individual, the spouses, the children, and all the people around them. It is we who witness a society of convenience at all costs: killing our own children when they are still unborn; killing our older relatives because we don't want to give them the care, the time, and the friendship that they need.[29]

Seeing the effects of the Culture of Death, young adults such as Lang are essentially saying, "We're not going to take it anymore."

[28] "Teenagers Are Becoming More Pro-Life Than Their Parents," New York Times, March 31, 2003.

[29] "Mary Ann Glendon on Today's University Students," Zenit, April 3, 2004.

Young and Catholic

She is not alone.

Among the new generation of pro-life advocates are young people such as seventeen-year-old Brandon White of McKinney, Texas. Active in the New Orleans–based father-and-son apostolate Kepha for the past six years, White has courageously witnessed and evangelized to peers about his Catholic Faith and the horrors of abortion. His involvement in the Dallas chapter of Youth for Life has led him to give numerous presentations to youth on fetal development and what happens during an abortion.

He isn't afraid to stand out in a crowd. He frequently wears T-shirts with pro-life messages. At Collin County Community College, where White takes concurrent college courses, fellow students stop to ask him about his shirts.

"One female student told him he was brave to wear a shirt that read 'Purity is Sexy,' " says White's mother, Debra. In 2002, White attended World Youth Day. While there, he did sidewalk counseling outside a Toronto abortion clinic.

In the face of *Cosmopolitan* magazine's constant promise of "great sex," rampant promiscuity, the threat of AIDS, and the prospect of legalized same-sex marriage, more and more young people are turning to John Paul II's vision of human dignity. One young man who is helping to unlock the truths regarding the Catholic understanding of the human person and sexuality is Christopher West.

∞

Go West, Young Man!

Christopher West is blazing a trail. Fortunately, it's one that has already been laid down for him, notably by Pope John Paul II. He is exploring the uncharted new frontier of the Theology of the Body.

West has come a long way from his wilder, younger days. In fact, he almost left the Catholic Church twelve years ago because of its teaching on contraception. Twenty-one and single, West decided that he would at least allow the Church to explain itself to him before bolting.

While he had heard what he calls the "whats" of Catholic teaching on sexuality, he didn't understand the "whys." Instead, he found society's answers far more appealing. Years of unchaste behavior forced him to grapple with serious questions about sexuality, and in the end he decided to study Scripture. In so doing, he "began to see that God created sexual union to reveal His eternal mystery to the world," says West.

Not long after, West remembers sharing his ideas with one of his sister's high school teachers. The teacher responded, "Oh, you must've read the Pope's *Theology of the Body*."

"No, what's that?" said West.

"You haven't read it?" she replied. "I would have thought you had. You're talking just like the Pope."

"I couldn't believe it," West recalls. "The Pope talks about sex like this?"

The next day, West ordered the original four-volume collection of the Holy Father's Wednesday audiences. Given between September 1979 and November 1984, these audiences make up a catechesis on the bodily dimension of human personhood, sexuality, and marriage in the light of biblical revelation.

"They changed the way I see the whole universe," says West. "I knew then that I would spend the rest of my life studying the Pope's Theology of the Body and making it accessible to others."

And that is just what West has done — speaking, writing, and teaching about the Pope's theology to anyone who is willing to listen.

West received his own call to "go west" during his last semester at the John Paul II Institute. Knowing that he would soon need to provide for his family, and seeking work in a diocese, West found a novel way of looking for a place to work.

"I loved to ski," says West, "so I thought it couldn't hurt to call Denver." West placed a random phone call and left a message in the Marriage and Family Life office's voicemail.

"I hung up thinking I wouldn't hear back," recalls West.

Much to his surprise, he received a call later that same day. As it turned out, the boss was in a meeting securing funding for a position when West called. "When I hung up the phone, I told my wife, Wendy, 'It looks like we're moving to Denver,' " says West.

West spent four years as director of the Office of Marriage and Family Life for the Archdiocese of Denver, using that time as a launching pad for his teaching, speaking, and writing career. Today he lives in Pennsylvania and serves as a visiting professor of the Theology of the Body at the John Paul II Institute in Melbourne, Australia, at St. John Vianney Theological Seminary in Denver, and at the Institute for Priestly Formation in Omaha.

As part of his work, he travels across the country speaking and is working to establish the Theology of the Body Summer Institute to train laypeople, priests and religious. In addition, West has produced several series of audiotapes on the Pope's teachings.

In addition to his speaking, West has also used his gift of writing to convey his message. His first book, *Good News About Sex and Marriage*, was published by Servant in 2000. He has since written *Theology of the Body Explained: A Commentary on John Paul II's "Gospel of the Body"*; *Theology of the Body for Beginners: A Basic Introduction to John Paul II's Sexual Revolution*; and *The Gospel of the Body*, a book that explains the Holy Father's addresses from start to finish and makes them accessible to a wider audience.

Working on the books, says West, has given him a much wider understanding of the Holy Father's theology.

"I've read through the Pope's addresses more than ten times," explains West. "But the Pope is talking about inexhaustible mysteries. There is always some new point of application that can be drawn from it."

West believes that a sexual counterrevolution is underway.

"We will not be tyrannized by a theology of false liberation," says West. He compares the Culture of Death to the Berlin Wall. "The Berlin Wall came down unexpectedly, but behind it was ten years of people standing up for their dignity saying, 'I will not be oppressed by this ideology.' In our lifetime we will see the collapse of the Culture of Death. The Culture of Life will rise up from its ashes."

He insists that if there is to be a great springtime of Christianity, the collapse has to come. "It cannot come if the domestic Church closes itself to the Holy Spirit, which is precisely what contraception does. There will be no springtime without a full return to the truth of the Christian sexual ethic. There will be no renewal of the Church in the world without a return to the fullness of marriage and family life," adds West.

In addition to his speaking and writing, West teaches the Pope's theology to seminarians.

"Eighty percent of the seminarians I teach are enthused. They wonder why they haven't heard this teaching before," says West. He admits, however, that for the other twenty percent, it's difficult to teach an old dog new tricks. "Those who have been classically trained in theology realize that the Holy Father is doing something novel," explains West. "They are not used to the Pope's approach and have a difficult time making sense of what he is saying."

Most seminarians embrace the teaching, says West, because it has immediate pastoral implications. "If we understand that the spousal relationship is an analogy for understanding the Christian mystery, all of the Church's controversial teachings — cloning, contraception, abortion, and women's ordination — fall into place and make sense. Each is a part of an indispensable whole. As soon as you remove one, the whole mystery collapses. This is why the dissent from *Humanae Vitae* has led us to the crisis in the Church today."

The Theology of the Body, he says, offers an answer to that crisis.

"For such a time as this have we been given the Theology of the Body," explains West. "We look at the sin of Adam, and the Church says, 'O happy fault!' We can look at the fault of the error of the sexual revolution that has won for us the Theology of the Body. It basically says to the sexual revolution, 'You have no clue how valuable sex really is.' "

∞

The Rise of Apostolic Lay Movements

Young adults strive for personal holiness, and they often look to community life for help. Ever since the Second Vatican Council, the Church has witnessed a tremendous growth in ecclesial lay movements. Taken collectively, these new ecclesial realities — such as Communion and Liberation, Community of Sant'Egidio, the Ecclesial Carmelite Movement, Emmanuel Community, Focolarini, the Neocatechumenal Way, Regnum Christi, Schoenstatt, and the charismatic renewal — represent millions of lay Catholics trying to live out their Catholic Christian Faith with others. The Holy Father has described these realities as "providential expressions of the new springtime." As such, they cannot be ignored.

While the movements are diverse in nature, they are drawing large numbers of young adults.

One example of such movements is the creation of the first Ecclesial Carmelite Movement in the United States. Started in July 2003 in Lincoln, Nebraska, the movement already has more than twenty members, most of them younger.

"The goal of the movement is to make the ancient Carmelite charism more available to the laity," explains Wally Boever, who works as an administrator with Holy Family Medical Specialties. Boever and his wife, Katy, are members of the movement. The group's "school of charism" meets twice a month for reading and prayer.

"Such movements are a means of proposing holiness as a way of life for everyone," adds Boever.

∞

Achieving Holiness through Daily Living

Another ecclesial reality that has drawn youthful Catholics is Opus Dei. The Church's only personal prelature, Opus Dei is organized like a diocese without boundaries. The prelate, like a bishop, responds personally to the Pope.

The prelature was founded by St. Josemaría Escrivá in Madrid, Spain, in 1928 to help people live by the Gospels in their daily activities. Active in sixty countries, Opus Dei was established in the United States in 1949 and has centers in thirteen states and the District of Columbia.

"In general, Opus Dei is pretty young," says Luke Mata, thirty-seven, who serves as national coordinator of youth activities in Manhattan. "If you look at the average age of people who are directors of Opus Dei centers, it is about thirty. That usually strikes people."

Every Easter, the prelature brings four to five thousand youth to Rome for an audience with the Pope.

"The young are attracted by other people with a love for the Church and the Pope," says Brian Finnerty, director of communications for Opus Dei.

The central idea of Opus Dei, or "The Work," as it is known, is to help people come closer to God in their work and daily lives.

"Everyone is called to be a saint," explains Mata. "That means putting a lot of love into whatever you're doing — whether it's your family, your work, your driving, or going to the store to buy groceries. Josemaría Escrivá used to say that if you don't find God in the ordinary things, you're not going to find Him."

The centers sponsor days of recollection, study circles, spiritual direction, summer camps, retreats, and other spiritual activities. Members also join with one another as well as with non-members to organize charitable, educational, and cultural efforts such as schools in Washington, D.C.; mission trips to Mexico, Guatemala, and India; and achievement programs for inner-city youth in Chicago.

There are approximately eighty-five thousand men and women in Opus Dei — three thousand of them in the United States. But Mata says that Opus Dei isn't concerned with numbers.

"We're interested in making a difference in a person's life — one person at a time," says Mata.

One person who is making such a difference is thirty-three-year-old David Holzweiss. Holzweiss is making a difference in the lives of young people in the Bronx, where he serves as administrator of the South Bronx Education Foundation.

Born into a poor peasant family in Korea, Holzweiss was sent to an orphanage in Seoul at an early age. After bouncing from one family to the next, he was brought to the United States at the age of five. At six, he was placed with the Holzweiss family in Stamford, Connecticut. At the age of ten, he was struck by the idea of divine providence without knowing what it was called.

"I figured that I was here for some reason," says Holzweiss. "I felt very fortunate to be alive."

Holzweiss started wearing a scapular, and at the age of fifteen started attending daily Mass and aggressively seeking a vocation. Feeling indebted to the country, Holzweiss enlisted in the Marine Corps ROTC program and studied physics at the University of Notre Dame. During his junior year, a philosophy professor first introduced him to Opus Dei.

"We had to keep a journal," recalls Holzweiss. "In going over the journal, the teacher said that it looked as if I was searching for spiritual direction and told me of an Opus Dei center located just off campus." Thus began his relationship with "The Work."

Following graduation, Holzweiss spent four and a half years in the Marine Corps. After that, he volunteered at the South Bronx Educational Foundation, eventually being offered a job as its administrator. The foundation is an after-school supplementary educational program fed by sixty area public and parochial schools. It serves approximately five hundred students, teaching them virtues, business ethics, and professional-skills development using advanced materials.

One of Holzweiss's projects was developing a database to help students track the use of their time. Based upon how they make use of their time, the foundation is able to make specific recommendations. Holzweiss has also developed a generic examination of conscience that students can use at the end of each day to help them to see whether they are meeting their goals.

Holzweiss's involvement in Opus Dei has helped him to find purpose in his life.

"Prior to Opus Dei, a lot of my life was compartmentalized," he says. "The Work has drawn out for me the unity of life. The spiritual life is the source of that unity."

That unity of life can be seen in Holzweiss's efforts both inside and outside the foundation. Outside the school, Holzweiss teaches catechism classes to a dozen students and assists at a local parish. He's formed Commitment to Christ in Community, a group of young men and women who study source documents of the Church, in order to help rejuvenate the life of their parishes.

"Through Opus Dei I have learned what divine filiation is," concludes Holzweiss. "An orphan, I have come to understand how God is Father."

In addition to bringing members closer to our heavenly Father, Opus Dei also works to connect sons with their earthly fathers.

"Father-son clubs all across the U.S. are helping fathers to realize that they are the primary instructors of their children," says Mata. "In a typical summer, we'll have about four hundred people go through our summer programs."

Although not affiliated with Opus Dei, one such father-son lay apostolate is the New Orleans–based Kepha.

∞

Reuniting Fathers and Sons

It's two o'clock in the morning. Fifteen-year-old Chris LaFleur and his father, Andrew, and a dozen other fathers and their sons, all dressed in purple T-shirts, kneel before the Son of God. All the men are tired, but it's a sacrifice they are willing to make. They're taking part in eucharistic adoration, otherwise described by the men as "Yawns for Christ." It's only one of the activities that characterize the growing father-son apostolate Kepha. The group's motto is "Play Hard, Pray Hard!"

The apostolate has sparked an interest among fathers looking for a way to bond with their sons. With members in six states, and interest in several others, the organization continues to grow, largely through word of mouth.

The idea for Kepha came to Brent Zeringue eight years ago.

"It was a one-year experiment," says Zeringue, a former educator and hardware-store owner. "I challenged a group of eight boys to learn Bible verses that defended specific Catholic doctrines each month, raise money for the pro-life movement, say morning prayers and the Divine Mercy Chaplet every day, and practice acts of self-mortification such as giving up sweets or taking a cold shower." In exchange for their sacrifice, Zeringue promised the original group a retreat to Colorado at the end of the year.

The eight boys not only succeeded in meeting the challenge, but their interest continued.

Today, the organization has about eighty active fathers and sons in Louisiana, Texas, Oklahoma, Florida, Mississippi, and New York. Fathers in North Carolina, Ohio, Pennsylvania, Massachusetts, and Minnesota have also expressed an interest in starting chapters.

Kepha is defined by five charisms — apologetics, brotherhood, charity, mortification, and prayer. The charisms are modeled after the lives of the group's three patrons, Bl. Mother Teresa of Calcutta, St. John Bosco, and Bl. Pier Giorgio Frassati.

In fact, Frassati, the young Italian saint, inspires several of the group's mottoes. These include "dynamic orthodoxy, infectious joy," "verso l'alto" ("to the top"), and the group's slogan, "The Brotherhood of the Iron Will." Frassati is quoted to have said, "I beg you to pray for me a little, so that God may give me an iron will that does not bend and does not fail in His projects."

The group hosts monthly father-son retreats that are often combined with first-Saturday eucharistic adoration.

Young and Catholic

In May 2003, twenty-three fathers and their sons held a retreat at St. Peter's Catholic Church on Staten Island. In addition to "Yawns for Christ," the members picketed an abortion clinic with the Franciscan Friars of Renewal, carried a cross in a silent procession to "The Grunt Padre" (Fr. Vincent Capadanno) monument, and played games such as an egg toss and dodge ball.

"It's something like a Catholic Boy Scouts, but the emphasis is spiritual," says Zeringue.

The boys, ranging in age from eight to sixteen, make morning prayer and either the Divine Mercy Chaplet or the Rosary part of their daily routine. The average age is thirteen. Six- to eight-year-old boys are active in the pre-Kepha group, Saints Squad.

Members routinely raise money for charitable causes and perform charitable works, such as serving meals at the soup kitchen run by the Missionaries of Charity in Baton Rouge. The group's constitution mandates that half the money the boys collect for their retreats must be donated to charity. In five years, the Kepha members have donated over $20,000 to charitable organizations.

In addition, the group is characterized by a love for the Holy Father. Their trademark T-shirts read, "Where Peter is, there is the Church" and *"Roma locuta, causa finita est"* ("Rome has spoken, the matter is finished").

In recent years, group members have made pilgrimages with the pro-life Crossroads team, have attended World Youth Day, and have been to Rome.

Although Kepha sometimes takes Zeringue and his sons away from home, Zeringue's wife, Karen, is very supportive.

"Brent was inspired to start a Catholic boys group that would be more than just about having fun," says Karen, a mother of nine.

She sees one of the primary fruits of the group as spiritual brotherhood. "I remember the times when Brent didn't have friends," explains Karen. "Now Brent has brothers. With these men, he can go and talk with any of them. They are all spiritually connected through prayer. If one of the men or their sons is having difficulty, they will offer him spiritual bouquets."

That brotherhood is present among the boys as well. Karen recalls a boy from Mississippi who had joined the group. "He told the others, 'I like Kepha because no one makes fun of me like they do at school,' " says Karen. "That is so beautiful."

Karen adds that the group has also been of benefit to her as a wife and mother. "The women get together for family events and have become good friends, too," says Karen.

Some members travel great distances. Brandon White regularly travels nine hours from McKinney, Texas, to New Orleans to participate in the retreats. White has seen many fruits from his involvement in Kepha. Among them he notes, "leadership, maturity, the brotherhood, and an improvement in my religious faith."

"Before Kepha I never really thought about my faith, or had a reason to think about it," says White. "Now I find that daily morning prayer and the Divine Mercy Chaplet have caused me to go deeper in my relationship with God."

What started in New Orleans is catching on elsewhere. Recent chapters have been formed in Oklahoma and New York.

Before the chapter was started in Oklahoma, Fr. M. Price Oswalt brought information about the group to Oklahoma City Archbishop Eusebius Beltran.

"His response was, 'You not only have my permission, but you have my blessing and prayers,' " says Fr. Oswalt, pastor of Sts. Peter and Paul Catholic Church in Kingfisher, Oklahoma.

Fr. Oswalt first met the group at a Couple to Couple League convention in June 2002. "They were all wearing purple T-shirts," says Fr. Oswalt, "and the more they spoke, the more I was impressed with what they were doing." Fr. Oswalt was even more impressed by the young men's commitment.

"We had a couple of meals at a restaurant together," explains Fr. Oswalt. "While we were eating chips and salsa, one of the teen boys mentioned that he had given up chips that week. Another one had given up soda, and it wasn't even Lent. I wondered what possessed these young men to do this when no one is doing this. It was interesting, and I wanted to learn more."

In October 2003, the Oklahoma chapter held its first retreat.

"We hoped to get at least twenty-five fathers and sons," recalls Fr. Oswalt. "We had eighty-seven." Fr. Oswalt served as the spiritual director for Kepha's Rome retreat and has been asked to become the program's national spiritual director.

Fr. Oswalt sees one additional benefit to the group. "These men are highly dedicated to the Gospel of Life and the Eucharist," he says. "One of the fruits we will see from Kepha is vocations."

Legionaries of Christ founder Fr. Marcial Maciel, when asked why the young are attracted to ecclesial realities such as the Legionaries and Regnum Christi, said, "People are too tired of ideas and abstract notions. When Christ, the Christ of the Gospel, true God and true man, is preached to people, especially young people, they feel captivated by the beauty of His message, by the fascination of His person."[30]

∞

Got Devotion?

The holiness of the young is particularly noticeable in their spiritual lives and their attraction to specific devotions.

[30] "About the Founder of the Legion of Christ and Regnum Christi," *Zenit*, July 8, 2003.

Br. Ken Apuzzo with the Brotherhood of Hope describes many young people as "spiritual orphans."

"The older generation says that they've had enough adoration, the Rosary, or regular Confession. They say, 'We've gone past that.' "

But Br. Apuzzo finds just the opposite among the youth.

"The previous generation is imposing its experience on the younger generation, but the young are interested in traditional practices and devotions because they've never had them," he adds.

"No one ever taught these things to me," says Constance Coxon. "I didn't receive a lot of catechesis and therefore didn't discover my faith in its fullness until I went on a retreat at the age of twenty-four. That was the first time that I heard things like 'You have a mission in life,' and 'God needs you.' "

According to Sherry Weddell, some young priests call this phenomenon the "Great Betrayal."

"A Dominican seminarian told me, 'My parents' generation knew this existed and withheld all of it from us. We've had to uncover it for ourselves,' " says Weddell.

Indeed, many of the formerly popular forms of piety that were abandoned following the Second Vatican Council — Forty Hours devotions, eucharistic adoration, Corpus Christi processions, consecration to the Sacred Heart of Jesus, and the Rosary — have witnessed a resurgence in popularity, particularly among young Catholics. The Church has also observed the creation of new devotions, such as the Divine Mercy Chaplet, the additional Stations of the Cross, and the new Luminous Mysteries of the Rosary.

George Weigel addresses the renewal of devotional life in the United States in his books and his speeches. He tells the story of the thirty students who gathered at Williams College, a secular university, following one of his talks, to pray the Rosary.

Weigel notes, "It's something they do each evening."

Another example is the Divine Mercy devotion.

"The Chaplet of Divine Mercy has become the vehicle by which many Catholics have come back to devotions," Weigel adds, quoting the Holy Father's expression that, "true devotion to the Mother of God is always Christocentric."

The popularity of personal prayer can be seen in the success of prayer magazines and devotionals such as the monthly prayer book *Magnificat*.

Prior to the Second Vatican Council, the Daily Office was prayed primarily by priests and religious. However, one of the renewals of Vatican II has been the practice of the laity joining in the "Divine Office." In the midst of their daily activities, more than 330,000, young and old alike, are doing so with the help of *Magnificat*. This abbreviated Liturgy of the Hours allows readers to integrate the Church's eucharistic life more completely into their everyday lives, even if they are unable to attend daily Mass.

Published in France, *Magnificat* was inspired by Pierre-Marie Dumont as a way to incorporate the Church's prayer into people's daily lives. Whereas the Liturgy of the Hours can be cumbersome to use, this monthly publication is a streamlined Liturgy of the Hours designed to fit in the pocket. The publication provides all of the liturgical and scriptural texts for daily Mass each day of the month along with morning and evening prayers, readings of lives of the saints, and scriptural meditations.

The original French edition has more than 150,000 subscribers. The German edition has 30,000. The U.S. edition, launched in December 1998, has more than 150,000.

One of its readers is Kathryn Mulderink of West Michigan. She first started using the prayer guide five years ago, at the age of thirty-three. She says that she has loved the publication from the very first time she picked it up.

"I especially like the fact that the articles are often focused on the current liturgical season, and the meditations refer to the readings or Gospel for that particular day," Mulderink says.

She adds that she is not alone in using it.

"I see many younger people, in their twenties, carrying it to Mass, and our pastor uses it himself, often quoting from the meditation during his homily," she says.

A homeschooling mother of seven and a secular Carmelite, Mulderink uses *Magnificat* at Sunday Mass and daily Mass when she can make it, and uses the daily meditation for her own morning meditation. The magazine allows her to "breathe with the Church by reading the Gospel and meditation, and know that I am being enriched according to the Lectionary." She describes that opportunity as profound.

She thinks that the publication fills a void.

"A lot of people want something richer. They want to see deeper, but don't know where to look. They want a regular prayer life, but they don't know how to do it," she explains. "*Magnificat* provides all that in bearable doses, all in one package."

She doesn't see the trend toward traditional devotions as young people wistfully looking back to "the good old days," but rather as a manifestation of a deep desire for authentic truth — "a yearning for the really profound things that allow us to live deeper, fuller human lives."

∞

Prodigal Sons and Daughters

Why are the young embracing such devotions? For some, the tragic events of September 11, 2001 played a profound role.

Young and Catholic

"The habits of Catholicism you are raised with can only carry you so far," says thirty-two-year-old Brian O'Rourke, a gifts fundraiser for a private school in Somerville, Massachusetts. O'Rourke describes his relationship with the Church prior to 9-11 as somewhat tenuous.

"There were plenty of places where I really struggled with what the Church teaches, but I said the Creed without the slightest hesitation," he explains.

While killing time in midtown Manhattan in November 2001, O'Rourke came across St. Patrick's Cathedral.

"When I walked in, I saw people lining up for Confession."

Blocks away, what was left of the World Trade Center buildings was still smoldering. O'Rourke admits that he hadn't been to Confession in nearly a decade.

"Just in case there's something to this, I better do it," thought O'Rourke.

"It's been at least ten years since my last confession," he told the priest in the confessional.

"Welcome back. It's great you're here. That's what matters," replied the priest.

After decades of decline, some priests and scholars have noted a modest revival of interest in Confession, particularly among the young.

"We have pretty solid lines, probably thirty kids on Sundays before Mass," says Fr. William Byrne, Catholic chaplain at the University of Maryland's College Park campus. He adds that many Catholic students are "tired of this subjective sense of right and wrong. It doesn't match what their hearts are saying."[31]

[31] Murphy, Caryle, "Confession Rite Evolves to Meet Changing Need," *Washington Post,* October 5, 2003, C1.

Twenty-four-year-old graduate student Amy Lemoine of Louis-
ville, Kentucky, has been active in college ministry for five years.
She senses a renewal of interest in the Church among her peers.

"Those I see coming into college are on fire," says Lemoine.
"There are an exceptional number of people my age who are inter-
ested in the Church. They want praise and worship. They love the
Eucharist and say the Rosary. We love to read G. K. Chesterton."

That puts her at odds with many of her professors.

*Graduate
student Amy
Lemoine, who
has been active
in college
ministry for
the past five
years, notes
a renewal of
interest in the
Church among
her peers.*

"They think we're naive," she says. "We don't want to throw
away the traditions of the Church. We're not an either/or generation. We're a both/and generation."

She surveyed fellow students at Spaulding University to gauge
their beliefs regarding the Real Presence of Jesus Christ in the Eucharist. The results, she says, weren't surprising.

"Those who were educated and were active in their faith believed in the Real Presence," she says. "Those who said they did
not believe didn't consider themselves faithful Catholics."

∞
One-on-One Time
with Jesus Christ

There can be no denying the increased interest in eucharistic adoration. According to The Real Presence Association, approximately seven thousand parishes — forty percent of the total in the United States — have some form of regular eucharistic adoration. Seven hundred have perpetual adoration, where the faithful volunteer to spend an hour with Christ each week around the clock, seven days a week.

"There is a youth eucharistic revolution happening," says Br. Apuzzo.

"I love eucharistic adoration," says twenty-eight-year-old stay-at-home mother, Nicole Stallworth. "There is nothing more awesome than the fact that God the Son loves me so much that He wants to share the same space as me through Communion and that He waits in physical form for me to visit Him in person. I used to wonder what it would be like to have an audience with the Pope, but it hit me one day that virtually anytime I want, I can have an audience with his 'Superior.' "

The Association of Students at Catholic Colleges (ASCC) hopes to reproduce that growth on college campuses. In 2003, the ASCC, a loose fraternity of Catholic student leaders who are struggling to build Christian campus life on America's Catholic campuses, launched their Eucharistic Adoration Campaign in concert with the Manassas, Virginia–based Cardinal Newman Society.

The campaign is in response to the contemporary student life found at too many Catholic colleges. That life mirrors the rampant sexual activity and high levels of alcohol abuse that are common among students at secular colleges.

The society sees their effort as a small but poignant step toward redirecting the attention of Catholic college students to what is central about the Catholic Faith.

"The major social controversies in this country — abortion, contraception, sexual activity, and homosexuality — touch all college-age Catholics," says Patrick Reilly, president of the Cardinal Newman Society. "Because they tend to get so caught up in those issues, they tend to lose focus on the central fact of their Faith. *Ecclesia de Eucharistia*, the Holy Father's 2003 encyclical letter, has called us to return our focus to what is central to our Catholic Faith."

In May 2004, the Cardinal Newman Society hired Cathal Magee to head up the campaign's efforts. The former president and founder of the Apostolate for Perpetual Eucharistic Adoration in Ireland, Magee was successful in having adoration established in more than six hundred parishes in Ireland and hundreds more elsewhere around the world.

"We plan to identify a couple of colleges where we will put effort into establishing model programs and get a sense of what the needs of students are," explains Patrick Reilly, president of the Cardinal Newman Society. "Then we'll take those model programs and replicate them elsewhere." Reilly hopes eventually to bring adoration to non-Catholic colleges as well.

The Cardinal Newman Society has already identified fifty Catholic college campuses that have eucharistic adoration monthly, weekly, or during Lent, although still very few have perpetual eucharistic adoration.

Reilly wrote that students from the University of Notre Dame have seen the fruit of twice-weekly adoration.

"I know from stories that upperclassmen have relayed to me that the Catholic identity at Notre Dame has been undoubtedly strengthened since eucharistic adoration was implemented," says sophomore Christina Dehan. "I know it has changed the lives of many students here, and the very presence of Christ on campus can be felt on the days when He is exposed in the Blessed Sacrament."

The University of Notre Dame offers adoration every Monday and Tuesday from noon until ten p.m., drawing 140 students, faculty, and other employees with regular time slots.[32]

As assistant director of university ministry, Jesuit Fr. Will Prospero heads up eucharistic adoration at Marquette University in Milwaukee. It's something he started on campus since his arrival there four years ago. The first year, Fr. Prospero says that between three and four students would participate per hour.

In 2002, Fr. Prospero brought eighty students to World Youth Day in Toronto.

"Along the way, we had stayed overnight with the Sisters of Mary, Mother of the Eucharist in Ann Arbor," says Fr. Prospero. "I encouraged them to take time to visit the Blessed Sacrament during their stay. At 10:30 p.m. I walked into the adoration chapel, and it was just packed."

That experience was affirmed again at a Youth 2000 adoration event in Toronto. When the students returned to Marquette, he says, adoration really started taking off. In addition to silent adoration between noon and five p.m. on Mondays and Thursdays, during the 2003-2004 school year he added what he described as a "Holy Hour of Power" on Monday evenings at nine p.m.

The "Holy Hour" consists of praise music, reading the Sunday Gospel and reflection, a time of silent prayer, intercessory prayer

---

[32] Patrick Reilly, "College Students on Their Knees" *Lay Witness*, March/April 2003.

by the students, singing the Chaplet of Divine Mercy, and ending with the *Tantum Ergo*, Reposition, and the Divine Praises. Fr. Prospero describes the hour as a way for new students to be introduced to eucharistic adoration.

"They're not used to the silence, and some of them need more interaction," says Fr. Prospero.

Silent adoration now draws approximately six students per hour for an average total of between thirty and forty. The "Holy Hour" has been drawing increasing numbers of students, hovering around an average of twenty.

Fr. Prospero explains that it's not simply a matter of the young embracing the traditions of the Fifties, but that they are discovering them and making them their own.

"Young adults are embracing traditional devotions in their own way," says Fr. Prospero. "It's speaking to them."

He adds that adoration has had another unforeseen benefit.

"Whenever there is authentic prayer and devotion, there is fruit," says Fr. Prospero. "I've given direction to seven young women and two young men who have entered religious life over the past two years. All of them were actively involved in eucharistic adoration."

Vincent Strand is one of them. A twenty-one-year-old junior from Dousman, Wisconsin, he has experienced first-hand the transformation that comes through eucharistic adoration.

"Much of my foundation has come from my parents," says Strand. "They taught me what it meant to be a good moral person. There was never a question of whether or not we would attend Mass every Sunday, and we prayed before meals and before bed each night."

While home for the summer after his freshman year in college, Strand often played basketball at his local parish. While there, he made short visits to the sanctuary to pray. That was where he first stumbled upon eucharistic adoration.

"One time when I walked in, adoration was going on," says Strand. "As soon as I walked in, it was a moment of conversion. I felt the Lord speak to me. There was a real sense of the eternal that I hadn't previously experienced outside of Mass."

He compared his time of prayer in adoration before Christ in the Blessed Sacrament to being in Heaven for a short period. He says that adoration has not only deepened his relationship with Jesus Christ, but it has also led him to attend daily Mass more often.

"I'm meeting Jesus Christ in a way that I can't in any other way outside of Mass," he adds. "It has improved the intimacy of my relationship with Jesus Christ and has increased my attendance and my love at Mass. When I sit there in adoration, I hunger to receive our Lord in the Eucharist at Mass as well. I experience Mass differently now. I find that I can move to a depth of prayer that I wasn't able to previously. A eucharistic mentality is very much part of my spirituality now.

"We see the role that eucharistic adoration has played in the lives of so many saints. There is a mystery to it. It's completely different from so many of the other things that we do in our life. There is substance there."

Strand isn't alone. Many of his friends attend adoration or the Holy Hour of Power each week.

"There is a sense among my generation to get back to some of the historical roots of our Faith. There is a yearning for a more contemplative experience," explains Strand. "I grew up Catholic, but didn't experience a lot of these Catholic devotions, so when I did, it was like a breath of fresh air in my devotional life."

Strand's faith has also had a significant impact upon how he lives his life. He resides in an off-campus intentional Catholic community that was started by students several years ago. Known as the Catholic House, Strand resides there with six other men.

"We pray the Liturgy of the Hours together every morning at seven a.m., attend Mass at least once on a weekday, and have meals in common," says Strand. "It's a general atmosphere of college men trying to live out our discipleship in communion with the Lord."

There are presently two such houses for women, and one for men. The houses have also served as a place of discernment and a breeding ground for religious vocations, and several of the residents are considering or have entered religious life.

Strand is among them. Upon graduation in May 2005 he is considering the possibility of entering a religious order.

∾

The Path to Sainthood

Why are the young rejecting the prevailing cultural messages?

They do so because the Church offers something the world does not. Among faithful young Catholics, there is a sincere desire for personal holiness. At World Youth Day in Toronto, John Paul II told the young, "Do not wait until you are older to set out on the path of holiness. Holiness is always youthful."

"The Church's teachings are both demanding and sane in an insane world," says Donna Marie Joan Lewis, a thirty-two-year-old administrative clerk from Pittsburgh. "I can't see any other way of being Christian as logical. I can't really begin to describe how devastating not being Catholic would be for me since the only other option would be leaving Christ completely, and how can one describe the loss of the Infinite?"

There is an understanding among youth that such holiness requires sacrifice. In making such sacrifices, the young draw upon the lives of the saints in their daily walk with Christ. They recognize how desperately the current culture needs individuals who are willing to imitate the saints.

There are plenty to choose from.

The Church has officially recognized more than twelve thousand martyrs for the Faith in the last century alone. In addition, Pope John Paul II has beatified 1,330 and canonized 476 saints since the beginning of his pontificate, more than all his predecessors combined. He recognizes that in an age marked by unbelief, the young need modern examples of holiness. He has provided such examples, particularly through the canonization of many young saints. They include two of the Church's youngest canonized saints, Francisco and Jacinta Marto, the visionary children from Fatima. They also include Bl. Andrew the Catechist, the Vietnamese teenager martyred in 1644; Bl. Kateri Tekakwitha, the young Native American girl who embraced the Church; and the Italian mountain-climbing jokester Bl. Pier Giorgio Frassati.

Thirty-three-year-old Peter Braam of Denver credits Pier Giorgio Frassati and World Youth Day for his rediscovery of his Catholic Faith. At World Youth Day 1993 in Denver, Braam decided to use the event to make some money.

"I had a cardboard cut-out of the Pope that I set up on a street corner," recalls Braam. "I was taking photographs of people standing next to the cut-out."

A lifelong Catholic and self-described entrepreneur, Braam says that the event was a turning point for him.

"My whole life had been about making my ideas work," he says. "I realized how selfish my ambitions were. I realized that I had to submit my own dreams to the Holy Spirit and pray and listen, not just forge ahead. I understood that I needed to make my job God's instrument."

Four years ago, Braam started a Pier Giorgio Frassati group as a means of gathering faithful young adults for prayer, evangelization, service, and retreats. The group, says Braam, exploded from a handful of people to seventy. The effort also led Braam to a job as coordinator of young-adult ministry for the Archdiocese of Denver, a position he held until 2003.

His work with the Frassati group continues. The group has not only grown, but has evolved into the first International Frassati Festival — a weeklong event including Catholic speakers, hiking, stargazing, bonfires, and an outdoor concert. The festival was held at Camp St. Malo in Estes Park during the last week of June 2004. The event was attended by more than four hundred young adults from as far away as Canada and Italy.

Braam says that Frassati's example speaks particularly to those in their twenties and thirties.

"I identify with his strengths and weaknesses," admits Braam. "He had an interest in organizing events to bring people together to learn more about Christ. Like Frassati, we use the mountains as the place to do that. Our goal is to emulate the life of Pier Giorgio Frassati. He had a youthful spirit, and we identify with that."

Catholic motivational speaker Matthew Kelly admits that he draws inspiration from several saints in his life and work. He cites "St. Francis for his simplicity, St. Thomas More for his ability to move amidst worldly affairs and keep his virtue, and St. John Vianney for his simple and heroic holiness in shepherding people."

Twenty-two-year-old actress Lindsay Younce not only longs to be a saint, but she has also played one on film. Younce portrays Thérèse of Lisieux in the 2004 motion picture *Thérèse*.

She feels that saints such as Thérèse have a particular appeal to the young.

Young and Catholic

"Scripture speaks about the young not being taken seriously because of their age," says Younce. "For Thérèse, no one believed that she had a calling to be a nun, except for her father. She knew at age fifteen, and died at age twenty-four. She was young all of her life, and yet she had an incredible devotion to God and is a Doctor of the Church.

"The young often feel as if they have no responsibilities," Younce says. "They are given reasons to have a lack of direction, and when they do have a dream or a sense of God's will, they are not taken seriously. That happened to Thérèse as well, but she never gave up."

Younce identifies with Thérèse's experience. Despite a non-Catholic upbringing, she desired to convert to Catholicism at the age of seventeen.

"I knew that I wanted to be Catholic, but was told that I was too young to make such a decision," she says. "Thérèse, too, was told to wait to enter the convent, and the wait was worth it. So often we speak of the young as our future, but they are our present. We need to give them responsibilities, trust them, and let them follow their dreams."

"The formation in the domestic Church is through families who have known John Paul II since they were little and are now having children of their own," says Youth for the Third Millennium's Paul Bernetsky. "This is where the new springtime is coming from. They are the future of our Church — the saints in our midst. The whole face of the Church is going to change."

Peter McFadden agrees. He recalls sitting in the field on the final day of World Youth Day in Toronto.

"I hadn't showered, and we had been rained on," explains McFadden. "It wasn't the most comfortable feeling in the world." Then McFadden thought of the Pope.

"There he was, wearing all of his garments. It was warm and rainy. I realized that he probably wasn't comfortable either." It dawned on McFadden that the Holy Father didn't *have* to be there.

"Half the world was predicting that he wouldn't come," adds McFadden. "The reason he came in the condition he was in was because he wanted to tell us something." As a result, McFadden says that he listened to the Holy Father as he had never listened to him before.

"He asked *us* to be salt for the earth. There's nothing but good work to do," concludes McFadden. "It's a great time to be young and Catholic."

∞

Conclusion

The Seeds Are Sprouting

"The more I learn about my Faith,
the more I realize that it is well thought out,
logical, and deeply spiritual."

Rita Fitzgerald, 22, chemical engineer, Dallas, Texas

꩜

When a seed first takes root, the new plant emerges from the soil with force. The spindly growth bends and reaches desperately for the light. The growth, at this stage, can easily be destroyed by too much or too little sunlight, or too much or too little water. With proper care, however, the seedling will grow strong, producing much fruit.

The Church's New Springtime is at hand. Its seeds have been planted and have taken root. The new growth is just now emerging. That growth is evident from the stories told within this book. The young and young adults are searching for *the* Light. Our task is to help them find it.

If all these stories demonstrate one thing, it is that there is no single answer to the question of how the young are being drawn to and engaging with the Church. It is a mystery. The Holy Spirit continues to work much as He did when He fell upon a young Jewish girl in Nazareth more than two thousand years ago.

There have been, and continue to be, many avenues to Christ and His Church. Some seek refuge from broken homes. They find Jesus through prayer, devotions, or adoration. Some have been wounded by the empty lies of the media, and they hunger for the truth. They find Jesus through reading or a study group. Some have floundered from job to job, yearning for more meaningful lives. They question what God is asking of them. They are brought to Christ through a clearer understanding of their unique, God-given charisms and vocation. Still others are lonely. They are brought to Jesus by the Holy Spirit working through a parent, religious, friend, or stranger. Some are brought to Christ in their weakness. Convicted by their own sinfulness, they are drawn to Jesus' offer of forgiveness. In the arms of the Church and its sacraments, they can be made white as snow. They are attracted by beauty, goodness, and truth.

In *Tertio Millennio Adveniente*, the Holy Father wrote, "Christ expects great things from young people. . . . Young people, in every situation, in every region of the world do not cease to put questions to Christ: they meet Him, and they keep searching for Him in order to question Him further. If they succeed in following the road which He points out to them, they will have the joy of making their own contribution to His presence in the next century and in the centuries to come, until the end of time: 'Jesus Christ is the same yesterday, today, and forever.' "[33]

These stories demonstrate that the Holy Spirit is active and working, even when it might appear otherwise.

We are not called to despair, but to hope. To despair is to give up on God.

The many men and women in this book have not given up on Him. They have embraced Him with their arms wide open, willing to follow Him wherever He might lead.

Their example of fidelity should fill us with tremendous hope for the future of the Church.

---

[33] Pope John Paul II, *Tertio Millennio Adveniente*, 58.

∞

Resources

∞

TEEN MINISTRIES
Catholic Youth Foundation
731 Fieldstone Ln.
Elizabethtown, PA 17022
www.catholicyouth.org/

Catholic Youth World
Network
www.cywn.net/

Dead Theologians Society
National Headquarters
810 Pearl St.
Chippewa Falls, WI 54729
715-720-1524
www.dtsroom.com
celtdrums@charter.net

LIFE TEEN Headquarters
1730 West Guadalupe Rd.
Mesa, AZ 85202
480-820-7001
Fr. Fred Gaglia, Priest Liaison
fgaglia@hotmail.com

NET Ministries
www.netusa.org/
ministry@netusa.org
National Catholic Youth
Conference
www.nfcym.org/

REACH Youth Ministry
P.O. Box 130
Cowiche, WA 98923-0130
509-678-8754
http://pages.prodigy.net/reachym/

Steubenville Summer
Conferences
1235 University Blvd.
Steubenville, OH 43952
800-437-8368
www.franciscanconferences.com/

Young Disciples Teams
www.fargodiocese.org/cef/YD/
youngdisciples@fargodiocese.org
701-356-7900

Young and Catholic

Youth 2000
USA National Office
6225 Boca Raton
Dallas, TX 75230
214-361-2581
y2000hou@swbell.net
www.youth2000usa.org

Youth for the Third
Millennium
7007 Bradley Blvd.
Bethesda, MD 20817
301-365-3205
www.ytm.org/
mission@ytm.org

MUSIC AND MUSICIANS
Catholic Music Network
www.catholicmusicnet-
work.com

The Contemporary Catholic
Artist Network Catholic
Jukebox
www.apostlemusic
.com/jukebox/

Contemporary Catholic
Music
www.newheartnew
voices.com/

Ceili Rain
Davis Dunbar
315-487-4122
booking@ceilirain.com
129 Hillcrest Rd.
Syracuse, NY 13219

Crispin
5124 Karen Dr.
North Richland Hills, TX 76180
817-498-4942
www.crispinmusic.org/
crispin@crispin.com

Greg Walton
P.O. Box 1736
Columbia, TN 38402-1736
931-840-5409
www.gregwalton.com/
info@gregwalton.com

HeartBeat Records
802 Pershing St.
Donnellson, IA 52625
319-835-9144
www.heartbeatrecords.com
Ronald@heartbeatrecords.com

Omegarock.com
www.omegarock.com/
omegarockdj@yahoo.com

Troubadour for the Lord
350 CR 248
Berryville, AR 72631
501-253-0256
www.troubadour
forthelord.com/

COLLEGE ORGANIZATIONS
Association of Students at
Catholic Colleges
10562 Associates Ct.
Manassas, VA 20109
703-369-0444
www.catholiccollege
students.org/
Ascc@catholiccollege
students.org

Brotherhood of Hope
194 Summer St.
Somerville, MA 02143
617-623-9592
www.brotherhoodofhope.org/
info@brotherhoodofhope.org

Cardinal Newman Society
10562 Associates Ct.
Manassas, VA 20109
703-367-0333
www.cardinalnewman
society.org/

Catholic Campus Ministry
Association
1118 Pendleton St., Ste. 300
Cincinnati, OH 45202-8805
888-714-6631
www.ccmanet.org/
info@ccmanet.org

COMPASS
P.O. Box 6811
Providence, RI 02940
800-541-8112
www.collegecompass.org/

Fellowship of Catholic
University Students
(FOCUS)
P.O. Box 1210
Greeley, CO 80632
970-336-9881
www.focusonline.org/

National Catholic
Student Coalition
45 Lovett Ave.
Newark, DE 19711
302-463-5538
www.catholicstudent.org/
ncsc@catholicstudent.org

Young and Catholic

The Newman Foundation
1007 1/2 South Wright St.
Champaign, IL 61820
217-384-5961
www.newmancenter.com/
institute/index.html

St. Mary's Catholic
Center
603 Church Ave.
College Station, TX
979-846-5717
www.aggiecatholic.org/

CATHOLIC COLLEGES
Aquinas College
4210 Harding Rd.
Nashville, TN 37205
615-297-7545
www.aquinas-tn.edu/

Ave Maria University
1025 Commons Cir.
Naples, FL 34119
877-283-8648
www.naples.ave
maria.edu/
admissions@ave
maria.edu

Benedictine College
1020 North Second St.
Atchison, KS 66002
913-367-5340
www.benedictine.edu/

Christendom College
134 Christendom Dr.
Front Royal, VA 22630
800-877-5456
www.christendom.edu/
info@christendom.edu

DeSales University
Center Valley, PA 18034
610-282-1100
www.desales.edu

Franciscan University
of Steubenville
1235 University Blvd.
Steubenville, OH 43952
www.franciscan.edu

John Paul II Institute for
Marriage and Family
415 Michigan Ave., NE
Washington, DC 20017
202-526-3799
www.johnpaulii.edu/
information@johnpaulii.edu

Our Lady of
Corpus Christi
1200 Lantana
Corpus Christi, TX 78469
361-289-9095
www.colcc.com/
colcc@juno.com

Our Lady of Holy
Cross College
4123 Woodland Dr.
New Orleans, LA 70131-7399
504-394-7744
www.olhcc.edu
admissions@olhcc.edu

Thomas Aquinas College
10000 N. Ojai Rd.
Santa Paula, CA 93060
800-634-9797
www.thomas
aquinas.edu

University of Dallas
1845 East Northgate Dr.
Irving, TX 75062
972-721-5000
www.udallas.edu/

**YOUNG ADULT
RESOURCES**
Catholic Adventures
International
7525 S. Utica Dr., #138
Littleton, CO 80128
Kevin@catholic
adventures.com

Catholic Underground
St. John the Baptist
(Lower Church)
670 Yonkers Ave.
New York, NY

The Colebrook Society
P.O. Box 26345
Fairview Park, OH 44126
www.colebrooksociety.com/

Contemporary Roman
Catholics
Holy Trinity Church
213 West 82nd St.
New York, NY 10024
212-496-4554
www.crcnyc.org/
crchtc@yahoo.com

Young and Catholic

International Frassati Festival
www.frassatisociety.org/
Festival2004/Festival
home.htm
Kansas City Catholic
Young Adults
913-541-2562
www.kcyoungadults.com/
events@kcyoungadults.com

Love and Responsibility
Discussion Group
917-846-3798
www.catholicculture.com/
peter@catholic
culture.com

National Catholic
Young Adult Ministry
P.O. Box 32253
Washington, DC 20007
202-298-8178
www.ncyama.org/
info@ncyama.org

Pure Love Festival –
Atlanta
www.davesloan.com/

St. Olaf Young Adults
215 South 8th St.
Minneapolis, MN 55402
612-332-7471
www.saintolaf.org/soya/

Theology on Tap –
New York City
www.totnyc.org/

Young Adult Ministry –
Archdiocese of New York
http://yamny.org/about.htm

Young Adult Ministry/
Theology on Tap
711 West Monroe
Chicago, IL 60661
312-466-9473
yam@yamchicago.org

**THEOLOGY OF THE BODY
RESOURCES**
Christopher West Online
www.christopherwest.com

Gift Foundation
www.giftfoundation.org/

Theology of the Body
International Alliance
(TOBIA)
Anastasia Northrop
tobia@theologyofthebody.net
307-635-4233

Theology of the Body
Resources
www.Theologyof
thebody.net

ONLINE RESOURCES
Ave Maria Singles
P.O. Box 942
Front Royal, VA 22630
www.avemaria
singles.com

BustedHalo.com
www.bustedhalo.com/
index2.htm

Catholic Exchange
P.O. Box 231820
Encinitas, CA, 92023
888-477-1982
www.catholic
exchange.com/

Catholic.net
432 Washington Ave.
North Haven, CT 06473
www.catholic.net
info@catholic.net

Catholic Online
P.O. Box 9686
Bakersfield, Ca. USA 93389
661-869-1000
www.catholic.org/

Catholic Scripture
Study
http://css.catholic
exchange.com/

Catholic Singles
www.catholic
singles.com/

Groundpickle.com
Truth Helps, Inc.
18165 Brightlingsea Pl.
South Bend, IN 46637
www.groundpickle.com/
info@groundpickle.com

Young and Catholic

Matthew Kelly
Foundation
2330 Kemper Ln.
Cincinnati, OH 45206
www.matthewkelly.org/
513-221-7700
info@matthewkelly.org

Monks of Adoration
1227 Horizon Rd.
Venice, Florida 34293
941-492-6122
www.monksof
adoration.org/
monkadorer@comcast.net

New Advent
www.newadvent.com

NextWaveFaithful.com
22226 Westchester Blvd.
Port Charlotte, FL 33952
941-764-7725
fax: 941-743-5352
www.nextwave
faithful.com
mail@nextwave
faithful.com

Onerock Online
P.O. Box 12593
San Francisco, CA 94112
info@onerock.com
www.onerock.com

St. Raphael.net Catholic
Singles
www.straphael.net/

Your Catholic Voice
P.O. Box 9248
Bakersfield, CA 93389
661-869-1000
www.yourcatholicvoice.org/
info@yourcatholicvoice.org

YouthApostles.com
P.O. Box 16370
Cleveland, OH 44116
www.youthapostles.com/

VOCATION DISCERNMENT
Archdiocese of Newark,
New Jersey – Vocations
171 Clifton Avenue
Newark, NJ 07104-0500
973-497 4365
www.rcan.org/vocation/
index.htm
platebri@rcan.org

Archdiocese of Omaha,
Nebraska – Vocations
Fr. Ralph O'Donnell
100 North 62nd St.
Omaha, NE 68132
402-558-3100
www.omahapriests.org/omaha
priestsorg/index.html
vocations@archomaha.org

Archdiocese of St. Paul-
Minneapolis, Minnesota –
Vocations
2260 Summit Ave.
St. Paul, MN 55105
651-962-6890
www.10000vocations.org/
twwilson@stthomas.edu

The Catherine of Siena
Institute
P.O. Box 26440
Colorado Springs, CO 80936
888-878-6789
www.siena.org
info@siena.org

Companions of the Cross
199 Bayswater Ave.
Ottawa, Ontario,
Canada K1Y 2G5
613-728-3175
www.companionscross.ca/
compcros@cyberus.ca

Diocese of Arlington,
Virginia – Vocations
Office of Vocations
200 N. Glebe Rd., Ste. 600
Arlington, VA 22203
703-841-2514
www.arlingtondiocese.org/
vocations/home.html
vocations@arlington
diocese.org

Diocese of Bridgeport,
Connecticut – Vocations
894 Newfield Ave.
Stamford, CT 06905
203-322-5331
www.bridgeportdiocese.com/
vocations.shtml
fatherwalsh@snet.net

Diocese of Charlotte, North
Carolina – Vocations
www.charlottediocese.org/
chancery@charlotte
diocese.org

Diocese of Fall River,
Massachusetts – Vocations
P.O. Box 2577
Fall River, MA 02722-2577
508-675-1311, ext. 109
www.fallrivervocations.org/
vocations@dioc-fr.org

Diocese of Lansing,
Michigan – Vocations
300 W. Ottawa
Lansing, MI 48933
517-342-2507

Diocese of Kansas City,
Kansas – Vocations
Catholic Church Offices
12615 Parallel Pkwy.
Kansas City, KS 66109
913-647-0356
www.archkck.org/
vocations/vocations.asp
fatherbrian@catholic.org

Diocese of Peoria,
Illinois – Vocations
Bishop Franz Center
613 NE Jefferson Ave.
Peoria, IL 61603
309-671-1569
www.cdop.org/vocations/
index.cfm
frbrownsey@cdop.org

Diocese of Rockford,
Illinois – Vocations
Rev. Aaron Brodeski,
Director of Vocations
Diocese of Rockford
P.O. Box 7044
Rockford, IL 61125
815-399-4300, ext. 396
www.rockvoc.org/
mail@rockvoc.org

Diocese of Wichita,
Kansas – Vocations
424 N. Broadway
Wichita, Kansas 67202
316-684-6896
www.cdowk.org/
vocations.htm

The Dominican Sisters
of St. Cecilia
801 Dominican Dr.
Nashville, TN 37228-1909
615-256-5486
www.nashville
dominican.org/
stcecilia1860@cs.com

Franciscan Friars
of the Renewal
St. Joseph Friary
523 W. 142 St.
New York, NY 10031
212-281-4355
www.franciscanfriars.com

Franciscan Sisters of
the Sorrowful Mother
P.O. Box 1042
Steubenville, OH 43952
740-544-5534
www.torsisters.com/
index2.htm
torsisters@juno.com

Legionaries of Christ
www.legionariesof
christ.org

Poor Clare Nuns of
Perpetual Adoration
Our Lady of the Angels
Monastery
3222 County Rd. 548
Hanceville, AL 35077
www.olamshrine.com/
olam/the_nuns.htm

Pre-Theologate at
Ave Maria College
Center for Discernment
300 W. Forest Ave.
Ypsilanti, MI 48197
734-337-4650
pretheo@avemaria.edu

Pre-Theologate at
Franciscan University
Fr. John Cody, C.Ss.R.
Franciscan University
1235 University Blvd.
Steubenville, OH 43952
740-283-6495
pretheo@franciscan.edu

Sisters of Life
198 Hollywood Ave.
Bronx, NY 10465-3350
718-863-2264
www.sistersoflife.org/

Young and Catholic

Sisters of Mary, Mother
of the Eucharist
4597 Warren Rd.
Ann Arbor, MI 48105
734-994-7437
www.sistersofmary.org/
smmevocations@rc.net

Society of St. John
Cantius
825 North Carpenter St.
Chicago, Illinois 60622
www.societycantius.org/
kolinskid@yahoo.com

Vocation.com
www.vocation.com

Western Dominican
Province
5877 Birch Ct.
Oakland, CA 94618-1626
510-658-8722
www.opwest.org/
vocations@opwest.org

**DEVOTIONAL
RESOURCES**
Magnificat Magazine
www.magnificat.net/
magnificat@devline.biz

The Real Presence
Association
7030 West 63rd St.
Chicago, IL 60638
773-586-2352
www.therealpresence.org/
qcs@therealpresence.org

ECCLESIAL REALITIES
Communion and Liberation
CL National Office
The Human Adventure
Corporation
420 Lexington Ave.,
Ste. 2754-55
New York, NY 10170-0002
212-337-3580
www.clonline.org/
clusa@clhac.com

Community of the
Beatitudes
2924 West 43rd Ave.
Denver, CO 80211
720-855 9412
www.beatitudes.us/
info@beatitudes.us

Community of
Sant'Egidio
www.santegidio.org/en/

Emmanuel Community
www.emmanuel
community.com/
info@emmanuel
community.com

Focolare
via Frascati 306
00040 Rocca di
Papa (Rome)
Italy
www.focolare.org/en/
sif@focolare.org

Kepha
205 Schexnaydre Ln.
Destrehan, LA 70047
www.kepharocks.org/
kepharocks@cnonline.net

NeoCatechumenal Way
www.camminoneo
catecumenale.it/en/

Opus Dei
330 Riverside Dr.
New York, NY 10025
212-532-3570
www.opusdei.org/
info@opusdei.org

Regnum Christi
www.regnumchristi.org/

Schoenstatt
www.schoenstatt.de/
index_english.htm

Sodalitium Christianae Vitae
(Christian Life Movement)
www.newevang.org/mvceng/
LucianeU@aol.com

Taizé Community
www.taize.fr/en/index.htm

Natural Family Planning
Billings Ovulation Method
Association USA
P.O. Box 16206
St. Paul, MN 55116
651-699-8139
www.boma-usa.org/
info@boma-usa.org

Young and Catholic

Couple to Couple League
P.O. Box 111184
Cincinnati, Ohio 45211-1184
513-471-2000
www.ccli.org/
ccli@ccli.org

Family of the Americas
800-443-3395
www.familyplanning.net/
index-home.html

NFP Outreach
3366 NW Expressway,
Bldg. D, Ste. 630
Oklahoma City, OK 73112
888-NFP-6383
www.nfpoutreach.org/
nfpoutreach@
nfpoutreach.org

One More Soul
1846 N. Main St.
Dayton, Ohio 45405-3832
800-307-7685
www.omsoul.com
omsoul@omsoul.com

Pope Paul VI Institute for the
Study of Human Reproduction
6901 Mercy Rd.
Omaha, NE 68106-2604
402-390-6600
www.popepaulvi.com/
popepaul@popepaulvi.com

CATHOLIC MEDIA
Ascension Press
P.O. Box 1990
West Chester, PA 19380
610-696-7795
www.ascensionpress.com/

Ave Maria Radio
www.wdeo.net/

Crisis Magazine
1814 1/2 N. St., NW
Washington, DC 20036
202-861-7790
http://mail@crisis
magazine.com

Eternal Word Television
Network
5817 Old Leeds Rd.
Irondale, AL 35210-2164
205-271-2900
www.ewtn.com

First Things
156 Fifth Ave., Ste. 400
New York, NY 10010
212-627-1985
www.firstthings.com/
ft@firstthings.com

Ignatius Press
www.ignatius.com

Immaculate Heart
Radio
P.O. Box 180
Tahoma, CA 96142
866-77-HEART
www.ihradio.org

National Catholic
Register
432 Washington Av.
North Haven, CT 06473
203-230-3800
www.ncregister.com

Our Sunday Visitor
200 Noll Plaza
Huntington, IN 46750
260-356-8400
www.osv.com

Relevant Radio
P.O. Box 10707
Green Bay, WI 54307-0707
www.relevantradio.com
info@relevantradio.com

Sophia Institute Press
Box 5284
Manchester, NH 03108
800-888-9344
www.sophiainstitute.com/
orders@sophiainstitute.com

Touchstone Magazine
The Fellowship of
St. James
P.O. Box 410788
Chicago, IL 60641
773-481-1090
www.touchstonemag.com/
tanner@touchstone
mag.com

Salt + Light Television
415 Yonge St., Ste. 900
Toronto, ON M5B 2E7,
Canada
416-971-5353-5353
www.saltandlighttv.org/

Young and Catholic

LifeSiteNews
301-104 Bond St. East
Toronto, ON M5B 1X9,
Canada
866-787-9947
www.lifesitenews.com/
lsn@lifesite.net

INTERNATIONAL
ORGANIZATIONS
Carnivale Christi
www.carnivalechristi.com/

Catholic Adult Education
Melbourne
278 Victoria Parade
East Melbourne, Victoria
3002 Australia
03 9412 3340
www.melbourne
.catholic.org.au/caem/
caem@melbourne
.catholic.org.au

Catholic Family and
Human Rights Institute
866 United Nations Plaza,
Ste. 427
New York, NY 10017
212-754-5948
www.c-fam.org/
c-fam@c-fam.org

JPII Institute Australia
278 Victoria Parade
East Melbourne Victoria 3002
03 9417 4349
www.jp2institute.org/
info@jp2institute.org

Sydney University
Catholic Chaplaincy
www.usydcc.org/

World Youth Alliance
847A Second Ave., #502
New York, NY 10017
646-796-3458
www.worldyouth
alliance.org/index.shtml
wya@worldyouthalliance.org

World Youth Day 2005 Cologne
http://www.wjt2005.de/

ABSTINENCE RESOURCES
National Abstinence
Clearinghouse
801 East 41st St.
Sioux Falls, SD 57105
888-577-2966
www.abstinence.net/
info@abstinence.net

Project Reality
1701 E. Lake Ave., Ste. 371
Glenview, IL 60025
847-729-3298
www.projectreality.org/

**MISCELLANEOUS
RESOURCES**
Act One: Writing for
Hollywood
1763 North Gower St.
Hollywood, CA 90028
323-462-1348
www.actoneprogram.com/
actone@fpch.org

Catholic Answers
2020 Gillespie Way
El Cajon, CA 92020
619-387-7200
www.catholic.com

Catholics United for
the Faith
International Headquarters
827 North Fourth St.
Steubenville, OH 43952
800-693-2484
www.cuf.org/
info@cuf.org

Tim Drake

∞

Award-winning author Tim Drake serves as staff writer with the *National Catholic Register* and *Faith and Family Magazine*. He has published more than six hundred articles in various periodicals and has appeared on Catholic radio and television programs. He resides in St. Cloud, Minnesota, with his wife and five children.

∞

Sophia Institute Press®